ZUNI JEWELRY

Theda and Michael Bassman

Photography by Gene Balzer

Revised and Expanded 2nd Edition

Schiffer Publishing Ltd

4880 Lower Valley Road, Atglen, PA 19310 USA

DEDICATION

To our children—Leslie, Gary and Jeff.

Title page photo:
Edith Tsabetsaye, one of the renowned Zuni artists, shown wearing pieces from her own collection. She excels in making needlepoint jewelry.

Top: Coral channel inlay necklace, earrings, bracelet, and ring of hummingbird design made by Annie Quam Gasper in 1998. Courtesy of Turquoise Village. $1500 set.

Bottom: All of this jewelry was made with turquoise snake eyes by the Haloo family in 1991. Courtesy of Turquoise Village. $54-$600

Revised price guide: 1999
Copyright © 1992 & 1999 by Theda and Michael Bassman.
Library of Congress Catalog Card Number: 99-62039

ISBN: 0-7643-0875-0
Printed in China
1 2 3 4

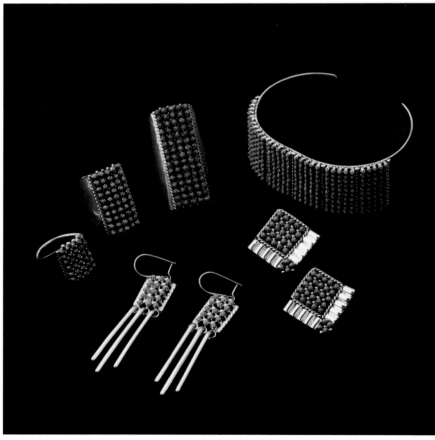

Published by Schiffer Publishing Ltd.
4880 Lower Valley Road
Atglen, PA 19310
Phone: (610) 593-1777;
Fax: (610) 593-2002
E-mail: Schifferbk@aol.com
Please visit our web site catalog at
www.schifferbooks.com

This book may be purchased
from the publisher.
Include $3.95 for shipping.
Please try your bookstore first.
We are interested in hearing from authors
with book ideas on related subjects.
You may write for a free printed catalog.

In Europe, Schiffer books are distributed by
Bushwood Books
6 Marksbury Avenue
Kew Gardens
Surrey TW9 4JF England
Phone: 44 (0)181 392-8585;
Fax: 44 (0)181 392-9876
E-mail: Bushwd@aol.com

CONTENTS

Bracelets made in 1991. **Row 1:** *(From left to right)* Inlay made of Chinese turquoise, coral, lapis lazuli, pink coral and melon shell by Robin Banteah. Inlay made of Chinese turquoise, lapis lazuli and coral by Duran Gasper. Inlay made of pink coral and lapis lazuli by Annie Gasper. Raised inlay hinged made of coral, turquoise, jet and lapis lazuli by Carol and Wilton Niiha. **Row 2:** Raised inlay made of coral and lapis lazuli by Roger Tsabetsaye. Inlay Sun God made of turquoise, coral, jet, gold lip mother-of-pearl and melon shell by Don C. Dewa. Inlay made of Chinese turquoise, pink coral and lapis lazuli by Duran Gasper. Inlay of 14-karat gold with pink coral, coral, sugilite and lapis lazuli by Ted Tsadiasi. **Row 3:** Inlay made of Chinese turquoise and lapis lazuli by Duran Gasper. Inlay made of turquoise, coral, pink coral, melon shell and jet by Olivia Panteah. Raised inlay made of coral, pink coral, turquoise, gold lip mother-of-pearl, lapis lazuli and melon shell by Lloyd Tsalabute. Courtesy of Gallup Inter-Tribal Indian Ceremonial. $180-$1200

ACKNOWLEDGMENTS

We would like to give our thanks to the many people who helped to make this book possible:

To Larry Linford for permitting photography of the jewelry on the busiest day of his life, preparing for the Gallup Inter-Tribal Indian Ceremonial.

To the entire staff at Turquoise Village who not only provided us with marvelous jewelry, but identification and names of artists as well, and especially to Ervina Soseeah, Joe Parent and Greg Hofmann.

To Priscilla Besselente who helped with the research. And to the following people who so graciously loaned us their jewelry to be photographed: Mary Benedict, Rosalyn Benitez-Bloch, The Gallup Inter-Tribal Indian Ceremonial personnel, Alissa and Ron Harvey, Roxanne and Greg Hofmann, Beverly Hurlbut, Martin Link, Leslie Newman, Edith Tsabetsaye, Gloria Tucson, Turquoise Village, Bryant Waatsa, Jr., Lorrayne Williamson, and the many private collectors who wish to remain anonymous.

To Gene Balzer, our wonderful photographer, who makes it all come alive.

The old Zuni Mission, now called Nuestra Señora de Guadalupe de Zuni in the village of Zuni dates back to 1629. In the 1960s, the Catholic Church, in cooperation with the Zuni Tribe and the United States National Park Service, began the process of excavating and rebuilding the mission. This work was finished in 1970. Subsequently, the National Endowment for the Arts gave Alex Seowtewa, an internationally known Zuni artist and muralist, a grant to begin work restoring the murals inside the church.

THE ARTISTRY OF ZUNI INDIAN JEWELRY

The Zuni Indians live in a village in New Mexico approximately thirty-five miles south of Gallup. Their reservation encompasses 409,182 acres and the population of tribal membership is 8,084. Of this number, approximately sixty-five percent of the tribal members, or 5,250, are involved in handcrafting jewelry. This activity provides their principal source of income. The remaining Zunis make their living from livestock, agriculture, other arts and crafts, tribal functions in government, limited local industry and some off-reservation employment.

Silversmithing was introduced to the Zunis approximately a hundred and twenty-five years ago by Navajo Indians and sometime before that by Spanish explorers and missionaries. Once learned, the Zunis fashioned their own techniques in jewelry making.

Zuni jewelry is made with sterling silver, with the exception of stone fetish necklaces and that which is labeled 14-karat gold. The use of stones and shells is particularly significant in Zuni designs while the silver is secondary, being the means by which the stones and shells are held in place and the preferred material for wire, decorative drops and ornamental balls.

In the making of fetish necklaces from turquoise, mother-of-pearl, coral, abalone, serpentine, ivory and shells, the artists carve likenesses of birds, bears, frogs and other animals. These delicate stone carvings are strung on strands of heishe which are usually made by Santo Domingo Indians.

Among the Zunis, both men and women wear an abundance of jewelry. Originally, the making of Zuni jewelry was a man's activity. Today, Zuni women also have become jewelry designers and makers. The women and men in some families collaborate, one doing the silver work while the other does the shell and stone cutting, inlaying and polishing. Other artists work alone, crafting the total piece. In addition, young people are learning the craft from their mothers and fathers. As techniques and skills are taught, the refinements are honed and frequently new designs are created by the "students". Contemporary Zuni jewelry reflects the efforts of the silversmith to express an artistic aspiration that will also be commercially satisfying and rewarding. The jewelry-making process adds to the richness of Zuni culture and heritage.

Zuni artists are world-renowned for their channel inlay patterns, fetish necklaces, cluster, needlepoint and petit point designs. They use stones, such as turquoise and pipestone, and incorporate silver, jet, lapis lazuli, malachite and shells brought by traders. Some of the more widely used and exotic shells include mother-of-pearl, coral, white clam, green snail, melon and pink shell. Their jewelry is meticulously crafted and their choice of colors in uniting stones and shells is remarkable in its correctness.

Earrings and pin/pendants made in 1998. **Row 1:** *(Left to right)* Turquoise, coral, mother-of-pearl, and jet inlay Knife Wing Dancer earrings made by Herbert and Esther Cellicion. Turquoise, coral, mother-of-pearl, and cowrie shell inlay owl earrings made by Pitkin Natewa. All of the following are pin/pendants: Turquoise, coral, mother-of-pearl, and jet inlay white owl made by Ann Sheyka. **Row 2:** Turquoise, mother-of-pearl, and jet inlay blue bird made by Andrea Shirley. Turquoise and black lip oyster shell deer made by Andrea Shirley. Turquoise, coral, mother-of-pearl, and jet inlay Knife Wing Dancer made by Betty Natachu. **Row 3:** Turquoise, pink shell, jet, and malachite inlay hummingbird with flower made by Andrea Shirley. Turquoise, coral, mother-of-pearl, and jet inlay dragonfly made by Wayne Haloo. Turquoise, coral, mother-of-pearl, and jet inlay bear made by Carol Seciwa. Turquoise, pink shell, yellow mother-of-pearl, coral, jet, and silver dots inlay parrot made by Loretta Gia. **Row 4**: Turquoise, coral, jet, azurite, gaspeite, blood-stone, green snail shell, denim lapis lazuli, lapis lazuli, and green turquoise inlay turtle made by Carmichael Haloo. Turquoise, mother-of-pearl, jet, and spiny oyster shell inlay Knife Wing Dancer made by Herbert and Esther Cellicion. Turquoise and coral snake eyes lizard made by Andres Hustito. **Row 5**: Turquoise, coral, yellow and white mother-of-pearl, jet, pink shell and cowrie shell inlay roadrunner made by Irene Edaakie. Yellow and white mother-of-pearl, penn shell, cowrie shell inlay owl made by Pablita Quam. Courtesy of Turquoise Village. $24-$225

The jewelry collected for this study reflects a broad cross-section of old and contemporary Zuni styles ranging from museum-quality pieces to those of everyday use. The world beyond the Zuni has discovered and popularized this jewelry, recognizing its beauty, careful workmanship and charm. The Zuni jewelry is dynamic, exquisite and truly an art form.

TERMS USED WITH ZUNI JEWELRY

Turquoise channel inlay made by Annie Quam Gasper in 1991. Courtesy of Turquoise Village. $1200 set.

Pin/pendants made in 1998. *Clockwise from top*: Coral cluster made by Alvina Quam. Turquoise needlepoint and teardrops made by Arvina Pinto. Coral cluster made by Lorraine and Luwayne Waatsa. Turquoise cluster made by Alice and Duane Quam. Turquoise rain cloud design with silver dangles made by Patrick Chavez. Coral needlepoint and teardrops made by Arvina Pinto. Center: Coral cluster made by Lorraine and Luwayne Waatsa. Courtesy of Turquoise Village. $105-$600

BEZEL—A thin strip of silver around a stone that is soldered to the silver base. It can be flat or saw-toothed.

BOLA TIE—A style of necktie with a jeweled silver slide strung on a lanyard having silver or jeweled ends.

CHANNEL INLAY—A design of shell or stone set with a silver bezel between each stone. The stones are sanded level and are polished.

CLUSTER—A group of large, tear-drop or round stones individually set.

CONCHA BELT—A belt made of silver and/or stones strung on leather or joined by silver links.

ETCHED INLAY—Ornamentation where a picture or design is etched into the surface of the stone or inlay.

FETISH—An object, usually of stone or shell, said to bring power and good fortune to its possessor.

HEISHE—Shell that has been cut, drilled and ground into round pieces and strung into a necklace. One strand may consist of several hundred pieces.

INLAY—Stones or shells ground flat on the top and level with the surrounding silver.

NEEDLEPOINT—An oval stone ground to fine points at both ends and set in a silver bezel.

PETIT POINT—An oval stone ground to a fine point at one end, rounded on the other end and set in a silver bezel.

RAISED INLAY—A style of inlay where the stone is rounded on the top instead of being ground flat.

SNAKE EYE—A series of very small, round stones, each of which is set in a bezel.

THE MATERIALS

Stones that are used in making Zuni jewelry. **Row 1**: *(From left to right)* Azurite, Malachite. **Row 2**: Jet, Serpentine. **Row 3**: Turquoise, Lapis lazuli, Pipestone.

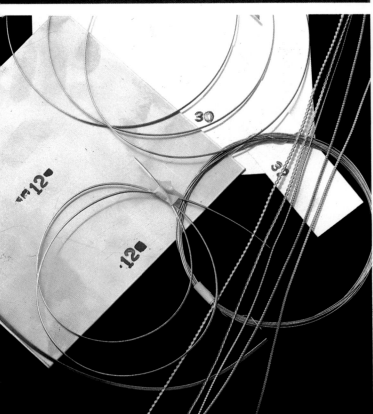

Shells that are used in making Zuni jewelry. **Row 1**: *(From left to right)* Green snail shell, polished; Green snail shell, unpolished; Abalone. **Row 2**: Red and pink coral. **Row 3**: Penn shell, Black lip oyster shell, Gold lip mother-of-pearl. **Row 4**: Melon shell, Cowrie shell, Pink shell.

Various sterling silver materials used in making Zuni jewelry.

THE MAKING PROCESS

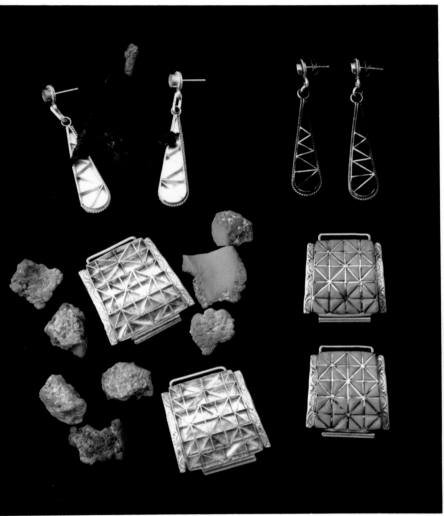

Raw turquoise is set on a stick with jewelry wax. The turquoise or coral is ground to the desired finish. The star is soldered on the silver plate. The silver ball in the center and the needlepoint bezels are also soldered on the plate. The turquoise or coral is set in the bezels and then the surplus silver is removed. The picture on page 42 shows the finished pin. Courtesy of Edith Tsabetsaye.

The unfinished watch tips and earrings on the left above have raised bezels on silver plates. Rough stones are ground, fit into the bezels and polished to desired smoothness. The finished earrings of jet and watch tips of turquoise are shown on the right above. Courtesy of Gloria Tucson. $45-$90, finished.

On the left is an unfinished necklace that Bryant Waatsa, Jr. is making. It shows how the turquoise is put into the bezels which have been soldered onto a flat silver plate. On the right is a finished turquoise needlepoint necklace, $390.

JEWELRY THROUGH
THE DECADES

Two inlay belt buckles made by Frank Vacit in the 1940s. The horse is made of turquoise, spiny oyster shell, jet and white clam shell. The eagle is made of turquoise, coral, jet and gold lip mother-of-pearl. The tooled leather belt was made by prisoners in the jail at Santa Fe. Courtesy of Beverly Hurlbut. $1200

The one-stone turquoise ring was made in the 1920s. The one-stone turquoise bracelet was put into pawn for $1.00 in the 1920s and was made by Willy Zuni. The bow guard was made before 1910. Courtesy of Beverly Hurlbut. $50-$500

Opposite page:
The Knife Wing Dancer necklace is made of turquoise and coral and is strung on silver beads. The earring and ring are good examples of petit point technique. The large petit point bracelet has a hundred and twenty-two turquoise stones. The narrow cluster bracelet has thirty-five turquoise stones, and the other cluster bracelet has eleven stones. All of this jewelry was made in the late 1930s and early 1940s. Courtesy of Martin Link. $125-$1500

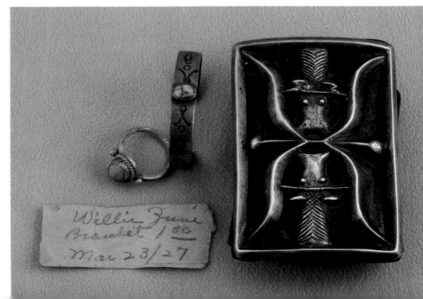

Inlay pin of Shalako Kachina design made of turquoise, coral, jet, spiny oyster shell, white clam shell, malachite and pink shell. Inlay pin designed as a Zuni altar is made of turquoise, coral, jet, white clam shell, pink shell and abalone. Both were made in the 1940s by Ralph Quam. Courtesy of Beverly Hurlbut. $1200-$1500

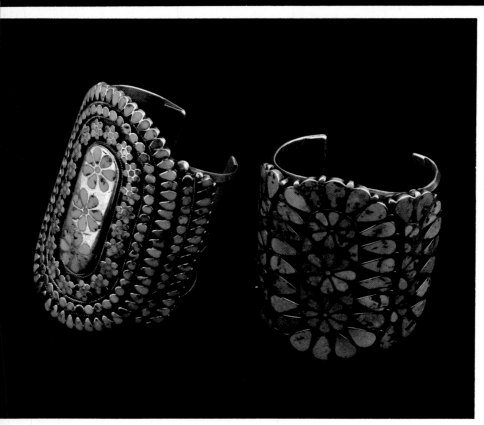

Opposite page:
A collection of pins and earrings made in the 1940s. The three inlaid butterflies on a chain were made of turquoise, coral and jet by Charlie Bitsue. The inlaid large Zuni Maiden was made of turquoise, coral, jet and mother-of-pearl by Della Case. The inlaid covered wagon was made by Virgil Dishta of turquoise, coral and mother-of-pearl with wheels that turn and a brake that moves. The one-stone tie bar in the shape of a tomahawk was made by Leekya Deyuse in the 1950s. Courtesy of Beverly Hurlbut. $50-$500

Left: The Sleeping Beauty turquoise inlay and needle-point bracelets were made by Virgil Dishta in the 1940s. Courtesy of Beverly Hurlbut. $1200-$1500

A collection of inlay rings. **Row 1**: *(From left to right)* Raised inlay Antelope Kachina made of turquoise, coral, penn shell, jet, mother-of-pearl and gold lip mother-of-pearl by Andrew Van Dewa in the 1970s. Raised inlay Antelope Kachina made of turquoise, coral, jet, mother-of-pearl, melon shell and serpentine in the 1970s by Velma and Don Dewa. **Row 2**: Raised and etched inlay Ram made with turquoise, gold lip mother-of-pearl and tortoise shell in the 1960s by Effie Qualo. Owl made of turquoise, coral, jet, white clam shell and abalone in the 1970s by Marita Sheyka. Raised inlay Antelope Kachina made of turquoise, coral, jet white clam shell and melon shell in the 1970s by Andrew Van Dewa. Raised inlay Mickey Mouse made of turquoise, coral, jet, mother-of-pearl and pink shell in the 1970s by Paula Lasiloo. All above courtesy of Mary Benedict. **Row 3**: Bird made of coral, jet and serpentine in the 1970s by Jack Mahke. Private collection. Turquoise Eagle Dancer made in the 1970s by Madeline Beyuka. Courtesy of Mary Benedict. Bird made of turquoise, jet and serpentine in the 1970s by Jack Mahke. Private collection. **Row 4**: Raised inlay Kachina figure made of turquoise, coral, jet, tortoise shell, gold lip mother-of-pearl and white clam shell in the 1960s by Frank Vacit. Courtesy of Mary Benedict. Man made of turquoise, coral, jet, pipestone and white clam shell in the 1970s by Madeline Beyuka. Courtesy of Mary Benedict. Zuni Maiden with pot made of turquoise, coral, jet, white clam shell, melon shell and gold lip mother-of-pearl in the 1970s by Madeline Beyuka. Courtesy of Mary Benedict. **Row 5**: Rainbow God made of turquoise, coral, jet and mother-of-pearl in the 1960s by Genevieve Tucson. Courtesy of Mary Benedict. Rainbow God made of turquoise, coral, jet and mother-of-pearl in the 1970s by Gillerimo Natachu. Private collection. Knife Wing Dancer made of turquoise, gold lip mother-of-pearl, coral, jet and white clam shell in the 1970s. Artist unknown. Courtesy of Mary Benedict. Rainbow God made of turquoise, coral, jet, mother-of-pearl and gold lip mother-of-pearl in the 1980s by Angela and Oliver Cellicion. Private collection. $45-$450

The turquoise needlepoint bracelets and hair pieces were made in the 1950s. Artist unknown. Courtesy of Beverly Hurlbut. $150-$250

RINGS

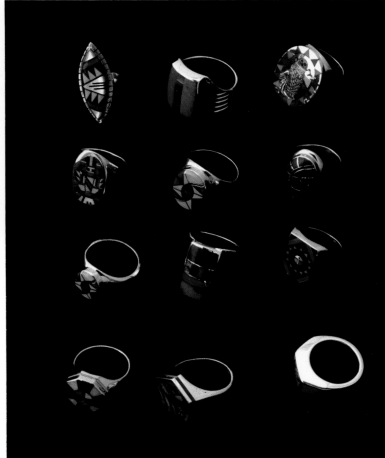

A collection of rings made in 1991. **Row 1**: *(From left to right)* Inlay in gold, made of mother-of-pearl, turquoise, coral, jet and gold lip mother-of-pearl by Viola Eriacho. Inlay of turquoise, coral and lapis lazuli. Made by Roger Tsabetsaye. Etched inlay owl made of mother-of-pearl, turquoise, coral and jet by Rolanda Coonsis. **Row 2**: Inlay in gold, Knife Wing Dancer made with mother-of-pearl, turquoise and coral by Pete Natachu. Channel inlay in gold made of coral and turquoise by Bailey Gia. Channel inlay in gold made of lapis lazuli by Dickie Quandelacy. **Row 3**: Channel inlay in gold made of coral and turquoise by Bailey Gia. Inlay made of turquoise, coral and lapis lazuli by Roger Tsabetsaye. Inlay in gold with raised Sun God made of coral, turquoise, jet and mother-of-pearl by Fred Natachu. **Row 4**: Inlay with Sun God made of mother-of-pearl, turquoise, coral and jet by Don Dewa. Inlay Knife Wing Dancer made of turquoise, spiny oyster shell, jet and mother-of-pearl by Rolanda Coonsis. Channel inlay made with turquoise, coral and lapis lazuli by Roger Tsabetsaye. Courtesy of Gallup Inter-Tribal Indian Ceremonial. $150-$975

A collection of rings made in 1991. **Row 1**: *(From left to right)* Raised inlay Thunderbird with Sun God made of turquoise, coral, jet and white clam shell by Faye and Larry Lonjose. Inlay made of green snail shell by Carol Laweka. Petit point of coral made by Vivian and Dirk Weahkee. **Row 2**: Inlay butterfly made of spiny oyster shell, mother-of-pearl and jet by Esther and Herbert Cellicion. Channel inlay of turquoise made by Lucille and Roger Leekya. Carved turquoise and coral made by Robert Eustace. **Row 3**: Channel inlay pink shell made by Anderson Toshewana. Inlay pink shell with raised turquoise flower made by L. Lasiloo. Inlay mother-of-pearl with raised turquoise flower made by Rodney Lasiloo. Channel inlay gold lip mother-of-pearl made by Wilmer Quandelacy. **Row 4:** Channel inlay pink shell flower with turquoise center made by Anselm Wallace. Channel inlay pink shell made by Anderson Toshewana. Channel inlay pink shell made by Stephen Siutza. Channel inlay pink shell band made by Carol Laweka. **Row 5**: Inlay mother-of-pearl, turquoise and coral made by Ron Harjo. Inlay and cluster made by Mary and Lee Weebothee. Needlepoint coral made by Beverly Weebothee. Courtesy of Turquoise Village. $30-$240

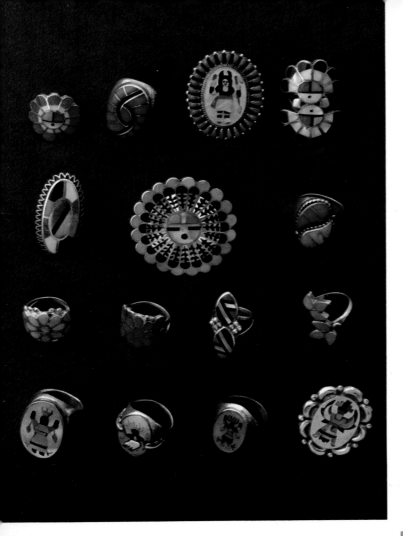

A collection of rings. **Row 1:** *(From left to right)* Inlay Sun God made of mother-of-pearl, turquoise and jet with coral tips in the 1970s by Lorinda and Larry Dickson. Private collection. Channel inlay of coral made in the 1970s by Amy and Dickie Quandelacy. Private collection. Inlay Kachina figure made of mother-of-pearl, gold lip mother-of-pearl, coral, jet and outer rim of coral petit point in the 1970s by Delfina Cachini. Courtesy of Mary Benedict. Inlay of double Sun God with eagle feathers made of mother-of-pearl, turquoise and coral with jet tips in the 1970s by S.L. Hattie. **Row 2:** Inlay made of turquoise, jet, spiny oyster shell and melon shell in the 1970s. Artist unknown. Courtesy of Mary Benedict. Inlay etched Sun God with turquoise tips made of mother-of-pearl, jet and coral in the 1970s by Pablita and Ed Quam. Courtesy of Mary Benedict. Channel inlay made of coral and turquoise in the 1970s by Jenny and Lloyd Salvador. Courtesy of Mary Benedict. **Row 3:** Channel inlay coved flower made of turquoise in the 1980s by Louise Siutza. Private collection. Channel inlay coved flower made of coral in the 1980s by Louise Siutza. Private collection. Inlay made of coral, jet and gold lip mother-of-pearl in the 1980s by Delberta Boone. Private collection. Channel inlay made of turquoise in the 1970s by Ben Eustace. Private collection. **Row 4:** Inlay Apache Mountain Spirit Dancer made of mother-of-pearl, coral, jet and turquoise in the 1970s by Tony Ohmsatte. Courtesy of Mary Benedict. Inlay Apache Mountain Spirit Dancer made of mother-of-pearl, coral, jet and turquoise in the 1970s by Tony Ohmsatte. Courtesy of Mary Benedict. Inlay Apache Mountain Spirit Dancer made of mother-of-pearl, coral, jet and turquoise in the 1970s by Tony Ohmsatte. Private collection. Inlay Apache Mountain Spirit Dancer made of mother-of-pearl, coral, jet and turquoise in the 1970s by Frank Vacit. Courtesy of Mary Benedict. $24-$300

A collection of inlay rings made in 1991. **Row 1:** *(From left to right)* Ring made of turquoise, coral, jet and mother-of-pearl by Cleo and Elcario Kallestewa. Ring made of turquoise, coral, jet and gold lip mother-of-pearl by Cletus Booqua. **Row 2:** Ring made of turquoise, coral, jet, mother-of-pearl and melon shell by Adeline Bowannie. Ring made of turquoise, coral, jet, mother-of-pearl and gold lip mother-of-pearl by Geraldine and Ricardo Terrazas. **Row 3:** Ring made of turquoise, coral, jet and mother-of-pearl by Geraldine and Ricardo Terrazas. Ring made of turquoise, coral, jet and mother-of-pearl by Jim Paywa. Courtesy of Turquoise Village. $36-$120

A collection of rings made in 1991. **Row 1:** *(From left to right)* Etched inlay eagle made of mother-of-pearl and jet by Nichelle and Derrick Edaakie. Etched inlay blue jay made of turquoise, jet, mother-of-pearl and malachite by Quinton Quam, Sr. **Row 2:** Etched inlay blue jay made of turquoise, jet, white clam shell, pink shell and malachite by Nancy and Ruddell Laconsello. Inlay hummingbird made of turquoise, coral, malachite, jet, mother-of-pearl, abalone and pink shell by Tracy Guardian and Edbert Booqua. **Row 3:** Etched inlay road runner made of jet, coral, mother-of-pearl and serpentine by Nichelle and Derrick Edaakie. Etched inlay spotted owl made of mother-of-pearl, abalone, jet and gold lip mother-of-pearl by Nichelle and Derrick Edaakie. Courtesy of Turquoise Village. $60-$150

Row 1: *(From left to right)* All made in the 1960s. Inlay ring with gold lip mother-of-pearl and tortoise shell. Artist unknown. Courtesy of Lorrayne Williamson. Inlay bracelet with mother-of-pearl, turquoise, coral and tortoise shell with Sun God insert. Artist unknown. Courtesy of Lorrayne Williamson. **Row 2:** Inlay ring of flower made of turquoise and tortoise shell by Rosita Wallace. Courtesy of Mary Benedict. Inlay ring of Antelope Kachina made of tortoise shell, mother-of-pearl, coral, jet and turquoise by Elizabeth and Adrian Wallace. Courtesy of Mary Benedict. Inlay coved ring of Sun God made of tortoise shell, jet, turquoise, coral and gold lip mother-of-pearl by Lorinda and Larry Dickson. Private collection. **Row 3:** Inlay, slightly coved Sun God earrings made of tortoise shell, coral, mother-of-pearl, jet and turquoise by Lorinda and Larry Dickson. Courtesy of Mary Benedict. Inlay coved Sun God ring made of tortoise shell, coral, mother-of-pearl, jet and turquoise by Lorinda and Larry Dickson. Courtesy of Mary Benedict. $25-$150

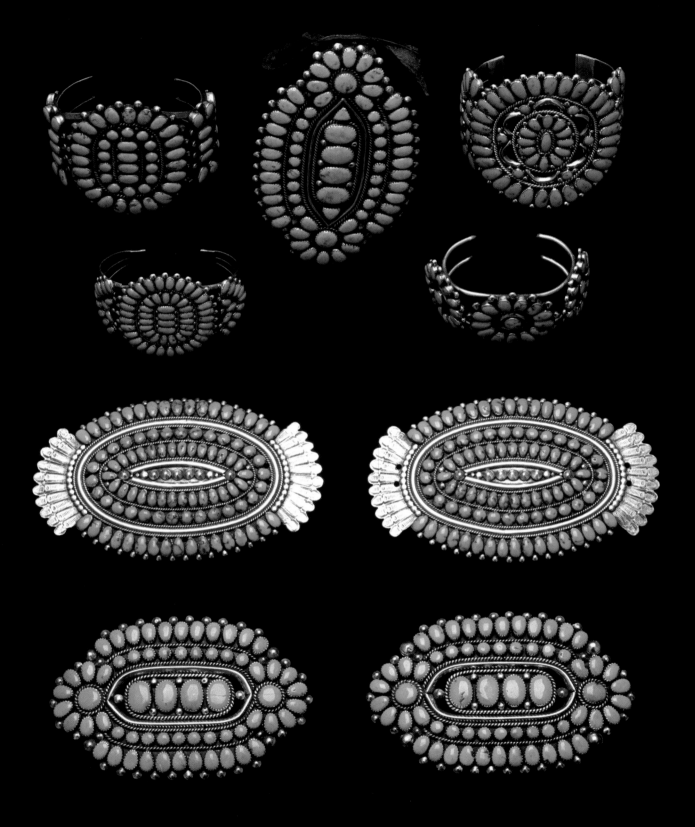

BRACELETS

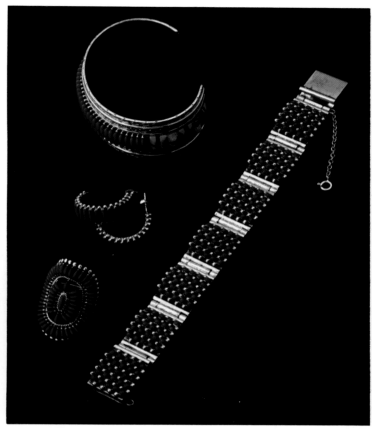

Opposite page:
A collection of pins and bracelets made of turquoise in cluster work. **Row 1**: *(From left to right)* Bracelet made of Kingman turquoise by Edith Tsabetsaye in 1973, from her collection. Bow guard made of Morenci turquoise by Edith Tsabetsaye in 1973, from her collection. Bracelet made of Sleeping Beauty turquoise by Alice Quam in 1991. Courtesy of Turquoise Village. **Row 2**: Bracelet made of Lone Mountain turquoise by Edith Tsabetsaye in 1968, from her collection. Bracelet made of Kingman turquoise by Edith Tsabetsaye in 1973, from her collection. **Rows 3 and 4**: Pins made of Kingman turquoise by Edith Tsabetsaye in 1972, from her collection. $300-$1500

Coral pieces made in 1991. Wide bracelet coral needlepoint and turquoise inlay. Made by Lloyd Tsalabute. Needlepoint earrings made by Calvin Eustace. Needlepoint ring made by Edith Tsabetsaye—First Prize winner. Snake eyes link bracelet made by Alice and Tom Hannaweeka—Second Prize winner. Courtesy of Gallup Inter-Tribal Indian Ceremonial. $180-$1150

A collection of bracelets made in 1991. **Left**: *(From top to bottom)* Channel inlay made of pink shell by Imogene Chopito. Channel inlay random pattern made of pink shell by Margie and Stuart Tucson. Channel inlay made of pink shell by Miranda Peynetsa. Inlay made of turquoise, coral, jet, pink shell, gold lip mother-of-pearl and turquoise by Rachael Weahkee. Channel inlay made of turquoise, coral, jet, pink shell, gold lip mother-of-pearl and grey oyster shell by Glendora and Rickell Booqua. Channel inlay made of turquoise by Louise and Stephen Siutza. Needlepoint made of turquoise by Calvin Eustace. Channel inlay made of coral by Angie and Elkus Gasper. Channel inlay made of coral, turquoise, jet and mother-of-pearl by Adeline Bowannie. Channel inlay made of turquoise, pink coral, lapis lazuli, melon shell and coral by Adeline Bowannie. Inlay made of turquoise, coral, jet and gold lip mother-of-pearl by April Seciwa. Inlay made of turquoise, coral, mother-of-pearl, jet and melon shell by Lena and Pat Tsethlikai. Raised channel inlay made of pink coral by Lucy Sheyka. Channel inlay made of pink coral by Philbert Chavez. **Right**:*(From top to bottom)* Raised channel inlay made of turquoise and gold lip mother-of-pearl. Artist unknown. Channel inlay made of jet, turquoise, coral and mother-of-pearl by Glendora and Rickell Booqua. Channel inlay made of pink shell with inlay Sun God made of turquoise, coral, jet, lapis lazuli and white clam shell by Carol and Delbert Seciwa. Channel inlay random pattern made of turquoise by Lola and Joe Hechilay. Channel inlay made of turquoise by Amy Wesley. Channel inlay made of pink shell and turquoise by Anselm Wallace. Courtesy of Turquoise Village. $60-$675

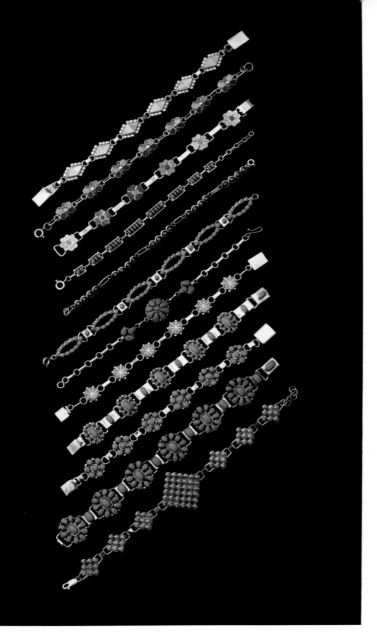

A collection of link bracelets made in 1991. *From top to bottom*: Inlay made of pink shell by Deborah and Anson Leekela. Inlay carved butterflies made of pink shell by Elva Quam. Inlay carved flower made of coral, mother-of-pearl, gold lip mother-of-pearl and turquoise by Nicholas Leekela. Needlepoint turquoise made by Connie and Alex Seowtewa. Snake eyes turquoise made by Sharon Hannaweeka. Turquoise made by Irma Waatsa. Cluster turquoise made by Beverly Weebothee. Channel inlay made of turquoise by Cordelia and Edmond Yatsattie. Turquoise made by Marie Basselente. Cluster turquoise made by FLS. Cluster turquoise made by Jane Passelente. Snake eyes turquoise. Artist unknown. Courtesy of Turquoise Village. $36-$225

Bracelets made in the 1960s. *Left*: Inlay Apache Mountain Spirit Dancer made of tortoise shell, gold lip mother-of-pearl, turquoise, mother-of-pearl and coral by Augustine A. Panteah. Private collection. *Center*: Inlay flower made of tortoise shell and turquoise by Rosita Wallace. Courtesy of Mary Benedict. *Lower center*: Inlay made of tortoise shell, turquoise, coral and mother-of-pearl. Artist unknown. Courtesy of Mary Benedict. *Right*: Inlay three-part link made of tortoise shell, turquoise, coral and mother-of-pearl. Artist unknown. Courtesy of Mary Benedict. *Lower right*: Inlay Sun God with eagle feathers made of tortoise shell, turquoise, coral and mother-of-pearl by Clara and Filbert Gasper. Courtesy of Mary Benedict. $150-$1200

FETISH NECKLACES

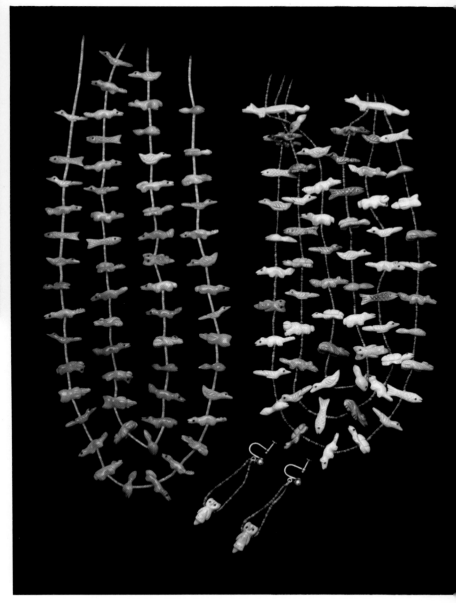

Left: Two-strand fetish necklace of twenty-nine birds made of abalone and red spiny oyster shell strung on olivella shell heishe by Emerson Quam in 1973. Courtesy of Mary Benedict. *Center:* One-strand fetish necklace of twenty-three birds and bears made of abalone, mother-of-pearl, red spiny oyster shell and serpentine strung on penn shell heishe by Emerson Quam in 1974. Courtesy of Mary Benedict. *Right*: Two-strand fetish necklace of thirty-four bears and birds made of serpentine, abalone, jet, mother-of-pearl, gold lip mother-of-pearl, and spiny oyster shell strung on olivella shell heishe by Emerson Quam in 1973. Courtesy of Rosalyn Benitez-Bloch. $250-$500

Left: Two-strand pink coral fetish necklace with sixty fetishes of squirrels, frogs, turtles, birds, tadpoles, owls, bears, rams and foxes strung on pink coral shell heishe. Made by Dinah and Peter Gasper in 1991. Courtesy of Turquoise Village. *Right*: Three-strand fossilized ivory fetish necklace with sixty-two fetishes of foxes, birds, fish, rams, turtles, owls, bears, tadpoles and frogs strung on olivella shell heishe with matching earrings. Made in 1986 by Dinah Gasper. Private collection. $1950-$3000

Three-strand fetish necklace with forty-five fetishes made of Mediterranean coral with matching earrings and 14-karat gold fittings. The fetishes are of bears, fish, turtles, frogs, tadpoles, squirrels and ducks. Made by Dinah and Peter Gasper and Andy Lee Kirk in 1991. This necklace took Best of Category for all Stone or Shell and was a First Prize winner. Courtesy of Gallup Inter-Tribal Indian Ceremonial. $4500 set.

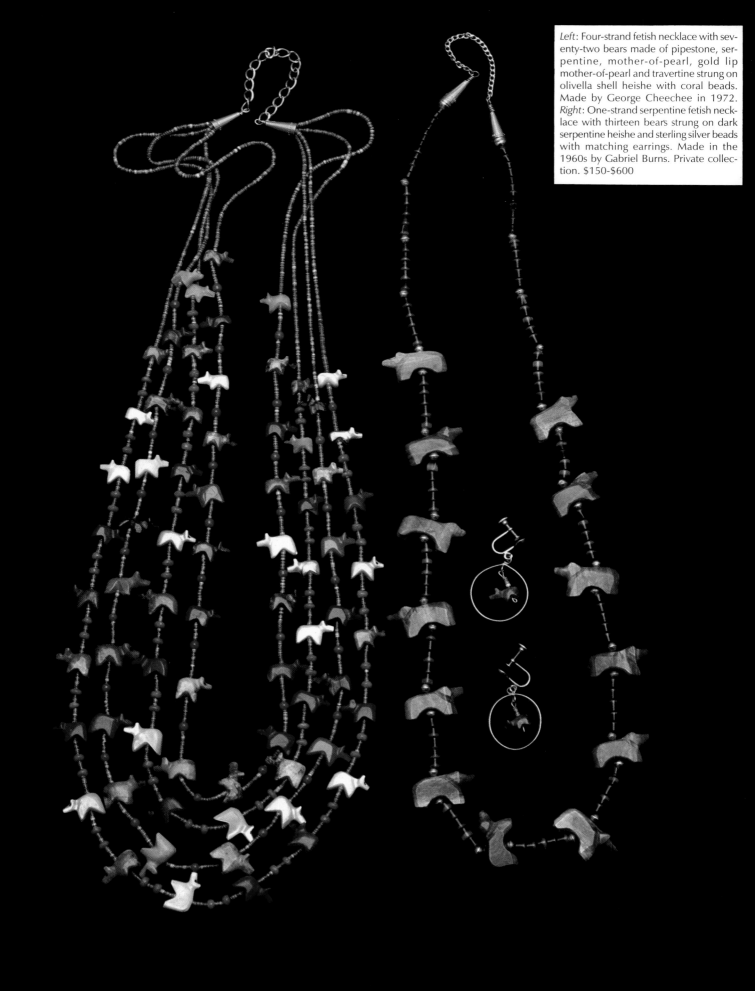

ACCESSORIES

Opposite page:
Eight fetish necklaces with two hundred and eight fetishes comprised of birds, foxes, squirrels, bears, fish and frogs strung on olivella shell, turquoise and pink coral heishe. The animals are made of spiny oyster shell, malachite, amber, green snail shell, pink shell, serpentine, jet, lapis lazuli, gold lip mother-of-pearl and melon shell by Lita and Sam Delena in 1991. Courtesy of Turquoise Village. $225-$500 each strand.

Money clips at *top*: Inlay Sun God with eagle feathers made of turquoise, coral, jet and mother-of-pearl by Clifford Bowannie. Inlay owl made of turquoise, coral, cowrie shell, jet and white clam shell by Velma Lesansee. *Left*: Raised inlay diamond shape made of coral, jet, turquoise and gold lip mother-of-pearl by Gladys and Leslie Lamy. Raised inlay of Thunderbird made of turquoise, coral, jet, white clam shell and gold lip mother-of-pearl by Sherry Niiha. Inlay Three Sun Gods made of turquoise, coral, jet and white clam shell by John Cheama. Key holder at left, inlay Sun God with eagle feathers made of turquoise, coral, jet and mother-of-pearl by Hubbard Soseeah. Channel inlay made of pink shell by Lorenda and Edison Bobelu. Inlay of Sun God made of turquoise, mother-of-pearl, coral and jet by Jenelle and Keith Waatsa. Channel inlay of turquoise, made by Lorenda and Edison Bobelu. Inlay Sun God with eagle feathers made of turquoise, coral, jet, gold lip mother-of-pearl and mother-of-pearl by Hubbard Soseeah. Courtesy of Turquoise Village. $12-$36

Hair pieces made in 1991. **Row 1**: *(From left to right)* Combs made with gold lip mother-of-pearl by Alberta and Gary Kallestewa. Combs made with spiny oyster shell by Alberta and Gary Kallestewa. **Row 2**: Barrette made of turquoise and coral by Angie Cheama. Combs made of turquoise and coral petit point by Vivian Tsethlikai. Barrette made of turquoise by Angie Cheama. **Row 3**: Combs of turquoise channel inlay by Helen Chopito. **Row 4:** Barrette of pink shell made by Alberta and Gary Kallestewa. Barrette of turquoise made by Alberta and Gary Kallestewa. Barrette of turquoise channel inlay made by Matthew Laiteyice. Red spiny oyster shell made by Alberta and Gary Kallestewa. Barrette of green snail shell made by Alberta and Gary Kallestewa. Courtesy of Turquoise Village. $24-$60

INLAY TECHNIQUES

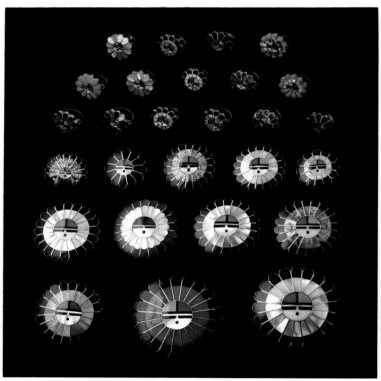

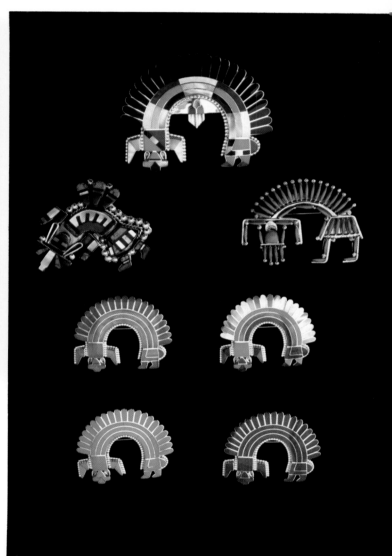

A collection of inlay rings and pin-pendants made by Sadie and Morris Laahty in the 1970s and 1980s. All are designed as Sun Gods. **Row 1:** *(From left to right)* Gold lip mother-of-pearl with turquoise, coral, jet and mother-of-pearl. Turquoise with jet tips, coral and mother-of-pearl. Tortoise shell with turquoise, jet, coral and mother-of-pearl, made in the 1960s. Cowrie shell with turquoise raised tips, coral, jet and mother-of-pearl. **Row 2:** Turquoise with coral, jet and mother-of-pearl. Mother-of-pearl with turquoise, coral and jet. White clam shell with jet tips, turquoise, coral and mother-of-pearl. Serpentine with turquoise, coral, jet and mother-of-pearl. White clam shell with raised turquoise tips, coral, jet and mother-of-pearl. **Row 3:** Coral with raised jet tips, turquoise and mother-of-pearl. Green snail shell with turquoise, coral, jet and mother-of-pearl. White clam shell with jet tips, turquoise, coral and mother-of-pearl. Cowrie shell with jet tips, turquoise, coral and mother-of-pearl. Abalone with turquoise, coral, jet and mother-of-pearl. Green snail shell with turquoise, coral, jet and mother-of-pearl. **Row 4:** Cowrie shell with jet tips, turquoise, coral, jet and mother-of-pearl. Jet with turquoise, coral and mother-of-pearl. Cowrie shell with jet tips, turquoise, coral and mother-of-pearl. Two with white clam shell with jet tips, turquoise, coral and mother-of-pearl. **Row 5:** Gold lip mother-of-pearl with jet tips, turquoise, coral and mother-of-pearl. Mother-of-pearl with serpentine tips, turquoise, coral and jet. Mother-of-pearl with jet tips, turquoise and coral. Abalone with jet tips, turquoise, coral and mother-of-pearl. **Row 6:** Pink shell with jet tips, turquoise, coral and mother-of-pearl. Coral with jet tips, turquoise, jet and mother-of-pearl. Mother of pearl with jet tips, turquoise and coral. Private collection. $60-$1000

Rainbow God pins made in 1991. **Row 1:** Inlay pin made with turquoise, coral, jet, pink shell, green snail shell, and gold lip mother-of-pearl by Fadrian Bowannie. **Row 2:** Inlay pin made of coral, jet, gold lip mother-of-pearl, mother-of-pearl and Chinese turquoise by Leonard Martza. Turquoise needlepoint pin made by Agnes and Hugh Bowekaty. **Row 3:** Inlay pin of pink coral made by Fadrian Bowannie. Inlay pin of turquoise, coral, mother-of-pearl, pink coral and malachite made by Fadrian Bowannie. **Row 4:** Inlay pin of turquoise made by Fadrian Bowannie. Inlay pin of coral made by Fadrian Bowannie which won Honorable Mention. Courtesy of Gallup Inter-Tribal Indian Ceremonial. $270-$600

Pins made in 1991. **Row 1:** *(From left to right)* Raised inlay Corn Kachina made of turquoise, coral, jet, malachite, gold lip mother-of-pearl and mother-of-pearl by Andrea Lonjose. Raised and etched inlay of a Zuni Maiden made of Chinese turquoise, gold lip mother-of-pearl, jet, spiny oyster shell and mother-of-pearl by Shirley and Virgil Benn. Inlay Knife Wing Dancer made of turquoise, coral, jet, green snail shell and gold lip mother-of-pearl by Pablita and Ed Quam. **Row 2:** Inlay and etched inlay of cardinal with flower made of turquoise, coral, jet, sugilite and mother-of-pearl by Nancy and Ruddell Laconsello. Inlay and etched inlay of blue bird with flower made of Chinese turquoise, spiny oyster shell and jet by Rolanda Coonsis. **Row 3:** Inlay and etched inlay of a toucan made in 14-karat gold with spiny oyster shell, jet, penn shell and turquoise by Nancy and Ruddell Laconsello. Inlay of Rainbow God and clouds made of turquoise, coral, malachite, spiny oyster shell and lapis lazuli by Rolanda Coonsis. Inlay and etched inlay of spotted owl made of turquoise, coral, jet and abalone by Nancy and Dennis Edaakie. **Row 4:** Inlay and etched inlay of Hano Clown made of turquoise, coral, jet, mother-of-pearl and black lip oyster shell by Nancy and Dennis Edaakie. Inlay of Rainbow God with turquoise, coral, jet, gold lip mother-of-pearl and lapis lazuli by Rolanda Coonsis. Courtesy of Gallup Inter-Tribal Indian Ceremonial. $225-$1200

Row 1: Inlay Rainbow God necklace made of turquoise, coral, jet and spiny oyster shell in the 1950s. Artist unknown. Courtesy of Mary Benedict. Inlay Sun God necklace with eagle feathers, made of turquoise, coral, jet and mother-of-pearl in the 1960s. Artist unknown. Courtesy of Lorrayne Williamson. **Row 2**: Channel inlay earrings made of turquoise in the 1960s by Janita and Sibert Kallestewa. Private collection. Inlay pin-pendant of an Antelope Kachina made of turquoise, coral, jet and mother-of-pearl in the 1970s. Artist unknown. Courtesy of Mary Benedict. Inlay pin-pendant of Apache Mountain Spirit Dancer made of turquoise, coral, jet and mother-of-pearl in the 1970s by Leonard Lonjose. Courtesy of Mary Benedict. **Row 3**: Inlay Sun God pin made of turquoise, coral, jet and mother-of-pearl in the 1960s by Elizabeth and Adrian Wallace. Private collection. Channel inlay earrings made of turquoise in the 1960s by Dena Toshowna. Private collection. **Row 4**: Raised inlay pin of Antelope Kachina made of mother-of-pearl, turquoise, coral, jet and white clam shell in the 1950s by Sybil Cachini. Courtesy of Mary Benedict. Inlay pin-pendant of Sun God made of pink shell, turquoise, jet, coral, mother-of-pearl and abalone in the 1960s by Eva and Dexter Cellicion. Private collection. Inlay pin-pendant of Sun God made of white clam shell, turquoise, coral and jet in the 1960s by Eva and Dexter Cellicion. Private collection. $75-$300

Opposite page:

Inlay squash blossom necklace of Rainbow Gods made in 1991 of turquoise, coral, jet and gold lip mother-of-pearl by Leonard Martza. Inlay and raised inlay Peyote Bird squash blossom necklace made of turquoise, coral, jet, white clam shell, black lip oyster shell and melon shell by Adeline Bowannie. Inlay choker made of pink coral and Chinese turquoise by Nancy and Sheldon Westika. Raised inlay and silver leaf necklace of Shalako Kachina and bear made of turquoise, coral, jet, gold lip mother-of-pearl, pink shell and green snail shell by Nicholas Leekela. Courtesy of Gallup Inter-Tribal Indian Ceremonial. $600-$900

Inlay Sun Gods made by Sadie and Morris Laahty. **Top row**: Ring, bracelet, watchband and belt buckle made of mother-of-pearl, coral, jet and turquoise in the 1970s. **Left**: Squash blossom necklace, earrings and link bracelet made of mother-of-pearl, coral, jet and turquoise in the 1970s. **Right**: Squash blossom necklace made in the 1960s. From top to bottom each Sun God is made of jet, cowrie shell, mother-of-pearl, tortoise shell, gold lip mother-of-pearl and abalone. The naja is of abalone, cowrie shell and tortoise shell. The face of the Sun Gods are made of mother-of-pearl, coral, jet and turquoise, as are the earrings. Private collection. $500-$2500

Row 1: Turquoise needlepoint bola tie with matching tips made of Lone Mountain turquoise in the 1980s by Edith Tsabetsaye. Courtesy of Roxanne and Greg Hofmann. Inlay and etched inlay pin of mountain lion made of turquoise, coral, jet and gold lip mother-of-pearl in 1979 by Ann and Porfilio Sheyka. Courtesy of Roxanne and Greg Hofmann. **Row 2**: Inlay pin in shape of a pot with bird, deer and flowers made of turquoise, coral and jet in 1991 by Nancy and Ruddell Laconsello. Courtesy of Turquoise Village. Inlay pin of rabbit made of turquoise, coral, jet, mother-of-pearl and black lip oyster shell in 1979 by Ann and Porfilio Sheyka. Courtesy of Roxanne and Greg Hofmann. **Row 3**: Raised inlay bracelet of coral made in the 1980s by Esther and Martin Panteah. Courtesy of Roxanne and Greg Hofmann. Raised inlay belt buckle of Apache Mountain Spirit Dancers made of green snail shell, turquoise, coral, jet, penn shell and gold lip mother-of-pearl in 1975 by Rosalie and Augustine Pinto. Private collection. Raised inlay bracelet made of turquoise, lapis lazuli and coral with the coral in the shape of corn in the 1980s by Rolanda and Harlan Coonsis. Courtesy of Roxanne and Greg Hofmann. $165-$3000

31

BOLA TIES

From left to right: Inlay Sun God with matching tips made of turquoise, coral, jet and mother-of-pearl in 1970 by Sadie and Morris Laahty. Private collection. Inlay Shalako Kachina made of tortoise shell, turquoise, coral, jet and mother-of-pearl in the 1960s by Paul Peyketewa, Jr. Private collection. Cluster made of Chinese spider web turquoise with matching tips in the 1980s by Lorraine and Luwayne Waatsa. Courtesy of Roxanne and Greg Hofmann. Cluster made of coral with matching tips in 1991 by Lorraine Waatsa. Courtesy of Turquoise Village. Inlay of Apache Mountain Spirit Dancer and Kingman turquoise cluster made of mother-of-pearl, turquoise, jet, coral and melon shell in 1973 by Edith Tsabetsaye, from her collection. $500-$1500

Opposite page:
Inlay squash blossom necklace with matching earrings and ring made of mother-of-pearl, turquoise, tortoise shell and coral in the 1960s by Lorinda and Larry Dickson. Courtesy of Mary Benedict. The ring on lower right is made of gold lip mother-of-pearl, turquoise, tortoise shell and coral made by the same artists. Private collection. $1000 set.

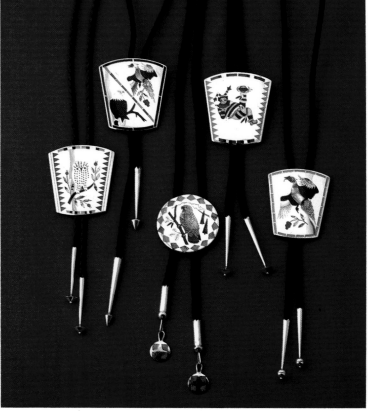

Opposite page:
A collection of bola ties. *From left to right:* Inlay of Knife Wing Dancer with matching tips made of turquoise, coral, jet, pink shell and mother-of-pearl in 1991 by Esther and Herbert Cellicion. Raised mosaic inlay with matching tips made of turquoise, coral, jet, abalone, mother-of-pearl, gold lip mother-of-pearl and penn shell by Ronnie Calavaza in 1991. This won an Honorable Mention in the Museum of Northern Arizona Zuni Show in 1991. Inlay and etched inlay of Bear Kachina made of turquoise, coral, jet, mother-of-pearl, gold lip mother-of-pearl, black lip oyster shell and malachite in 1989 by Andrea Lonjose. This won a Second Prize in the Gallup Inter-Tribal Indian Ceremonial in 1989. Inlay eagle made with turquoise, jet, mother-of-pearl, coral and gold lip mother-of-pearl by Janet Amesoli in 1991. Inlay and raised inlay of Longhorn Kachina made of turquoise, coral, jet, mother-of-pearl, serpentine, melon shell, spiny oyster shell and penn shell by Dexter Cellicion in 1991. Inlay and raised inlay of Shalako Kachina with matching tips made of turquoise, coral, jet, mother-of-pearl, gold lip mother-of-pearl, penn shell and pink shell by Beverly Etsate in 1991. Courtesy of Turquoise Village. $450-$900

Left to right: Raised inlay ring of Sun Kachina made of green snail shell, abalone, turquoise, coral, jet, mother-of-pearl, gold lip mother-of-pearl and pipestone in 1991 by Andrew Dewa. Courtesy of Turquoise Village. Raised inlay bola tie of Sun Kachina made of turquoise, coral, jet, mother-of-pearl, gold lip mother-of-pearl, abalone, pipestone and green snail shell in 1984 by Andrew Dewa. Private collection. Inlay and raised inlay bracelet of Sun God that is movable. Made of turquoise, coral, jet, gold lip mother-of-pearl, pink coral and mother-of-pearl in 1991 by Don Dewa. Courtesy of Turquoise Village. $450-$2000

A collection of bola ties made in 1991. *From left to right:* Inlay and etched inlay of spotted owl made of turquoise, coral, jet, mother-of-pearl and abalone by Nancy and Dennis Edaakie. Inlay and etched inlay of eagle and loon made of turquoise, coral, jet, mother-of-pearl and gold lip mother-of-pearl by Nancy and Dennis Edaakie. Inlay and etched inlay of eagle made of turquoise, coral, jet, green snail shell and abalone with matching tips by Rolanda Coonsis. Inlay of Hano Clown made of turquoise, coral, jet, mother-of-pearl and abalone by Nancy and Dennis Edaakie—Second Prize winner. Inlay and etched inlay pheasant made of turquoise, coral, jet, mother-of-pearl, abalone and penn shell by Nancy and Dennis Edaakie. Courtesy of Gallup Inter-Tribal Indian Ceremonial. $600-$900

Opposite page:
A collection of bola ties and one belt buckle. *From left to right*: Cluster bola tie and belt buckle made of coral and silver drops by Mary and Lee Weebothee in 1970. Private collection. Inlay Rainbow God made of turquoise, coral, jet and mother-of-pearl in 1970 by Lela and Roger Cellicion. Courtesy of Alissa and Ron Harvey. Turquoise channel inlay with matching tips made by Susie and Willis Leekity in 1970. Courtesy of Alissa and Ron Harvey. Inlay Hoop Dancer made of turquoise, coral, jet and gold lip mother-of-pearl in 1972 by Eddie Beyuka. Private collection. Inlay Plains Indians Dancer with silver drum tips made of turquoise, coral, jet and mother-of-pearl in the 1970s by Eddie Beyuka. Private Collection. Inlay Rainbow God with matching tips made of turquoise, coral, jet, abalone and mother-of-pearl in 1980 by Angela and Oliver Cellicion. Private collection. Inlay and raised inlay of Mountain Sheep made of turquoise, coral, jet, mother-of-pearl, black lip oyster shell, melon shell and serpentine in the 1970s by Velma and Don Dewa. Courtesy of Mary Benedict. $250-$1500

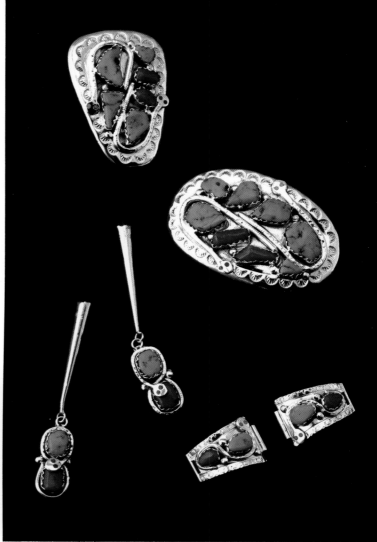

A matching set of bola tie with matching tips, a belt buckle and watch tips made of coral and Sleeping Beauty turquoise by Effie Calavaza in 1991. Courtesy of Turquoise Village. $500 set.

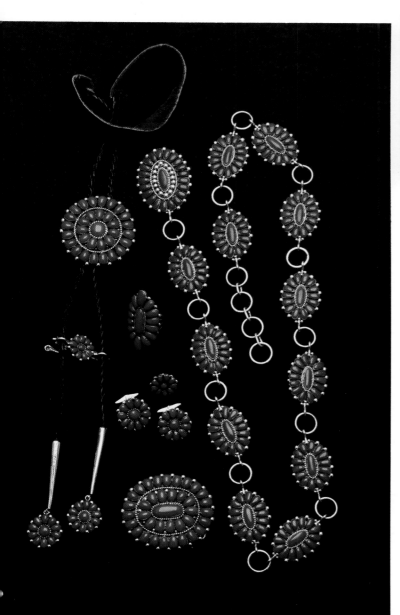

All coral clusters. *From left to right*: Bola tie and tie bar with matching tips, tie tac, cuff links and belt buckle made by Mary and Lee Weebothee in the 1980s. Courtesy of Roxanne and Greg Hofmann. Oval ring made in 1973 by Edith Tsabetsaye, from her collection. Concha belt with thirteen conchas made in the 1980s by Alice Quam. Courtesy of Roxanne and Greg Hofmann. $450-$4500

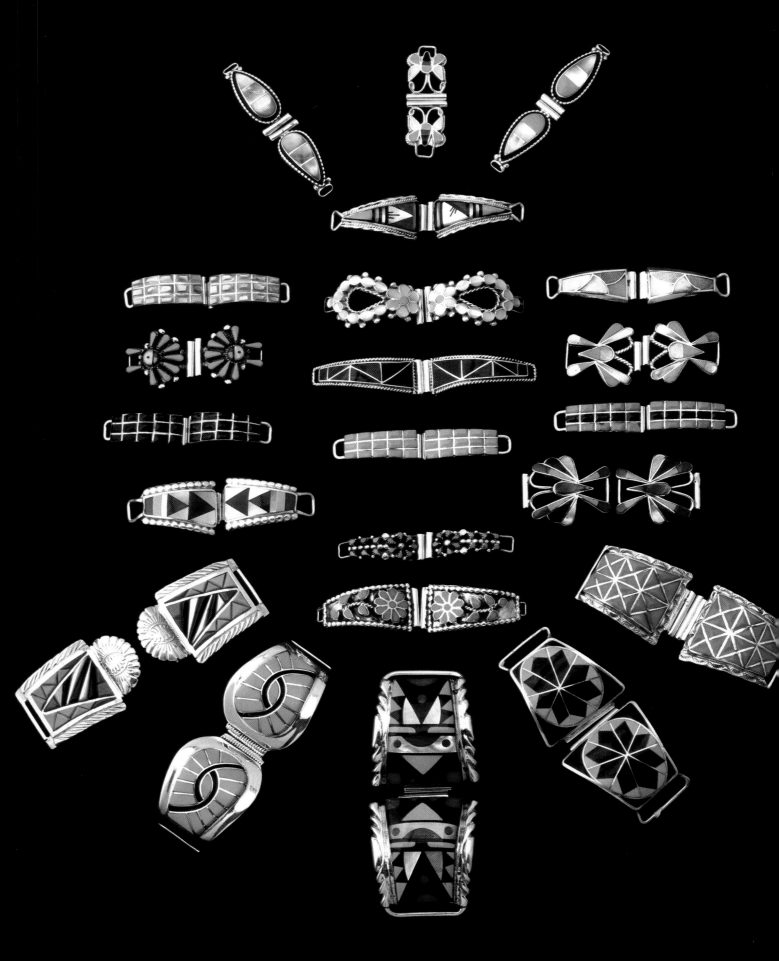

WATCHBANDS, WATCH BRACELETS AND BRACELETS

Watch tips 14-karat gold, made in 1998. *Upper:* Turquoise, coral, mother-of-pearl, and jet inlay made by Don and Viola Eriacho. *Center:* Turquoise channel inlay made by Rodney and Georgean Hughte. *Lower:* Turquoise nuggets made by Robert and Bernice Leekya. Courtesy of Turquoise Village. $750-$1500

Opposite page:
An assortment of women's and men's watch tips of inlay, raised inlay, channel inlay and needlepoint made in 1991. The following artists are represented by their work: Margaret and Solon Lalio, Virginia and Wayne Quam, Roberta Banketewa, Amy Wesley, Matilda and Valentino Banteah, Matthew Laiteyice, Ada and Ronald Yatsattie, Maryjane Edaakie, Zino Edaakie, Lilly and Charles Malani, Berdelle Tsikewa, Robert Dewa, Verenda Kallestewa, Marlene and Charles Booqua, Dion Leekity, Beatrice Laiteyice, and Susie and Willis Leekity. Courtesy of Turquoise Village $30-$375

Row 1: *(From left to right)* Bracelet of Kingman turquoise cluster and inlay of Apache Mountain Spirit Dancer made of turquoise, mother-of-pearl, jet and melon shell by Edith Tsabetsaye in 1973, from her collection. Inlay watch bracelet made of turquoise, coral and mother-of-pearl in 1970 by Jennie and Lloyd Salvador. Courtesy of Mary Benedict. Inlay bracelet made of turquoise, coral, jet, mother-of-pearl and gold lip mother-of-pearl in 1970 by Margie and Wilfred Eriacho. Courtesy Mary Benedict. Inlay bracelet made of turquoise, coral, jet and gold lip mother-of-pearl in 1970. Artist unknown. Courtesy of Mary Benedict. **Row 2:** Inlay watchband made of coral, jet and gold lip mother-of-pearl in the 1980s by Marylita and Alex Boone. Private collection. Inlay and raised inlay bracelet made of turquoise, coral, jet, mother-of-pearl and green snail shell in 1971 by Tony Ohmsatte. Private collection. Inlay link bracelet made of mother-of-pearl, turquoise, coral, jet and black lip oyster shell in the 1970s by RHB. Courtesy of Mary Benedict. **Row 3:** Inlay watchband made of turquoise, coral, jet and mother-of-pearl in the 1980s by Marlene and Charles Booqua. Private collection. Inlay watchband made of turquoise, coral, jet, mother-of-pearl and gold lip mother-of-pearl in 1988 by Marylita and Alex Boone. Private collection. Inlay watch bracelet made of turquoise, coral, jet and mother-of-pearl in the 1970s by Theresa Lus? Courtesy of Mary Benedict. $150-$750

Needlepoint necklace and earrings made of Lone Mountain turquoise by Edith Tsabetsaye in 1990. This was a First Prize winner at the Gallup Inter-Tribal Indian Ceremonial. Courtesy of Roxanne and Greg Hofmann. The needlepoint bracelet and ring are by Edith and from her personal collection. Earrings and necklace, $10,500. Bracelet and ring, $525.

Opposite page:
From left to right: Turquoise needlepoint three-part necklace and ring made in the 1970s by Janet and Dewey Ghahate. Courtesy of Alissa and Ron Harvey. Coral needlepoint bracelet and ring made in the 1980s by Eva L. and Raymond Wyaco. Private collection. $75-$300

NEEDLEPOINT AND PETIT
POINT TECHNIQUES

A group made of coral in 1991. *From top to bottom* Needlepoint pin made by Florinda and Norbert Haskie. Needlepoint pin made by Edith Tsabetsaye, a First Prize winner. (See page 9 which shows how the pin was made.) Cluster and petit point choker made by Lorraine and Luwayne Waatsa, a Third Prize winner. Petit point choker made by Glenda Eriacho. Courtesy of Gallup Inter-Tribal Indian Ceremonial.

Opposite page:
A group made of coral in 1991. *From top to bottom*: Needlepoint pin made by Florinda and Norbert Haskie. Needlepoint pin made by Edith Tsabetsaye, a First Prize winner. (See page 9, which shows how the pin was made.) Cluster and petit point choker made by Lorraine and Luwayne Waatsa, a Third Prize winner. Petit point choker made by Glenda Eriacho. Courtesy of Gallup Inter-Tribal Indian Ceremonial. $180-$1950

Row 1: *(From left to right)* Needlepoint coral link bracelet made in the 1980s by Josie and Garnet Owaleon. Private collection. Inlay and needlepoint watchband of domed Sun God made of turquoise, coral, jet and mother-of-pearl in the 1970s by Delfina Cachini. Private collection. **Row 2**: Carved turquoise link bracelet, watchband and ring made of Morenci turquoise in the 1970s by Linda Eustace. Private collection. Petit point coral ring and petit point turquoise ring made in the 1980s by Socorro and Vincent Johnson. Private collection. Petit point turquoise watchband made in the 1970s by Socorro and Vincent Johnson. Private collection. **Row 3:** Petit point turquoise choker in three parts made by Irma and Octavius Seowtewa in the 1970s. Private collection. Needlepoint turquoise bracelet made by Josie and Garnet Owaleon in the 1970s. Private collection. Needlepoint turquoise ring made by Horace Sanchez in the 1970s. Courtesy of Alissa and Ron Harvey. Needlepoint choker in three parts made in the 1970s by CJK. Petit point turquoise watchband Sun God design made of turquoise, coral, jet and mother-of-pearl in the 1970s by Delfina Cachini. Private collection. Inlay and needlepoint ring of domed Sun God made of turquoise, coral, jet and mother-of-pearl in the 1970s by Delfina Cachini. Private collection. $75-$450

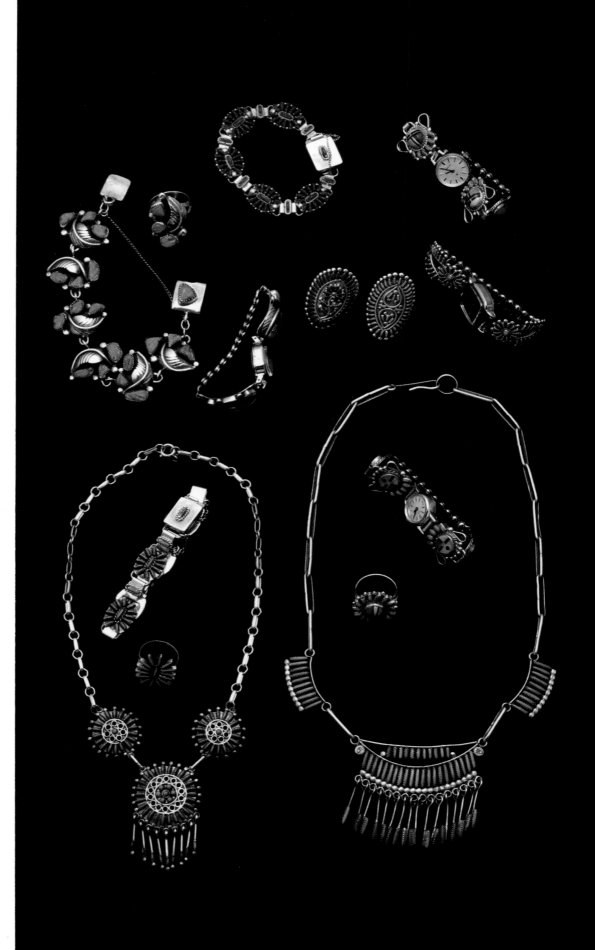

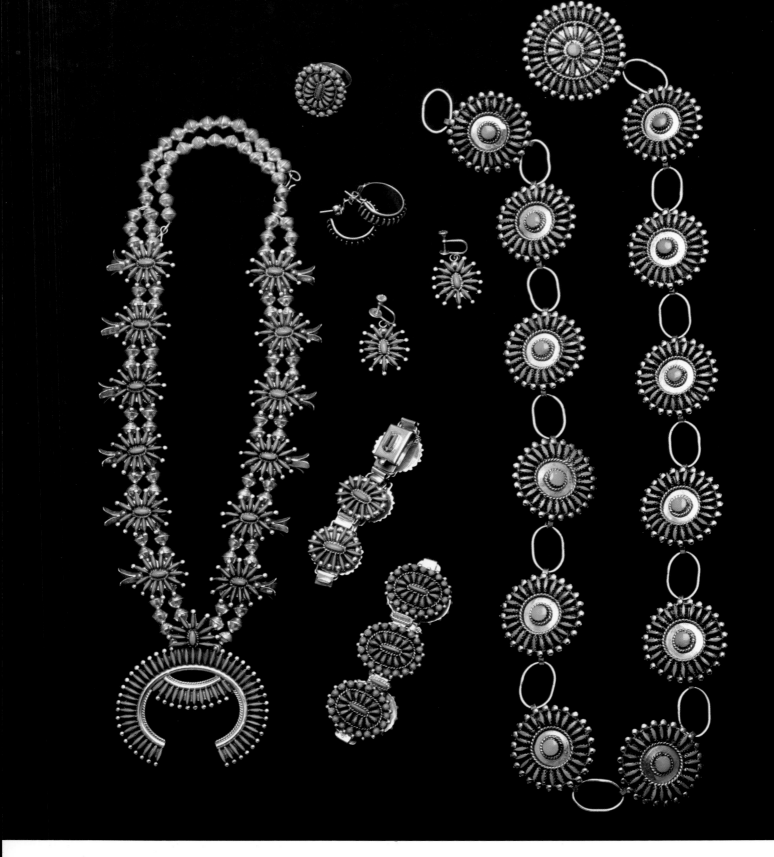

Turquoise jewelry made in the 1970s. *Left to right*: Needlepoint squash blossom necklace with earrings to match made by Agnes and Hugh Bowekaty. Private collection. Needlepoint and cluster ring made by Anita and Buddy Hattie. Private collection. Needlepoint hoop earrings. Artist unknown. Courtesy of Leslie Newman. Needlepoint link bracelet made by Rena and Evans Waatsa. Private collection. Needlepoint and cluster link bracelet made by Anita and Buddy Hattie. Private collection. Needlepoint concha belt with thirteen conchas made by Judy and Vernon Wallace. Private collection. $90-$1500

Group of fine jewelry made of turquoise. **Row 1:** Needlepoint coved ring made by Irma and Octavius Seowtewa in the 1980s. Private collection. Needlepoint oval ring. Artist unknown. Courtesy of Mary Benedict. Needlepoint ring made by Bryant Waatsa, Jr. in the 1980s. Private collection. **Row 2:** Snake eyes ring made by Pete Haloo in the 1970s. Private collection. Needlepoint ring made in the 1980s by Victoria Awelagte. Private collection. Needlepoint ring made in the 1970s by Eva Sanchez. Private collection. Needlepoint ring made in the 1980s by Bryant Waatsa, Jr. Private collection. **Row 3:** Earrings with dangles made in the 1980s by Arvina Sandoval. Private collection. Earrings made in the 1970s by Arvina Sandoval. Courtesy of Alissa and Ron Harvey. Needlepoint earrings made in the 1970s by Vernon Peynetsa. Courtesy of Alissa and Ron Harvey. **Row 4:** Petit point pin made in the 1980s by Donna Concho. Private collection. Needlepoint pin-pendant made in the 1980s by Eva L. and Raymond Wyaco. Private collection. Needlepoint pin-pendant made by Eva L. and Raymond Wyaco in the 1970s. Private collection. Needlepoint pin made in the 1980s by Rena and Evans Waatsa. Private collection. **Row 5:** Five needlepoint pin-pendants made by Lucille and Sampson Bowekaty in the 1980s. Private collection. **Row 6:** Needlepoint oval pin-pendant made in the 1980s by Agnes and Hugh Bowekaty. Private collection. Petit point round pin-pendant with dangles made in the 1980s by Irma and Octavius Seowtewa. Private collection. Inlay and petit point pin Knife Wing Dancer made of turquoise, coral, jet, gold lip mother-of-pearl and white clam shell in the 1970s by Delfina Cachini. Private collection. $25-$300

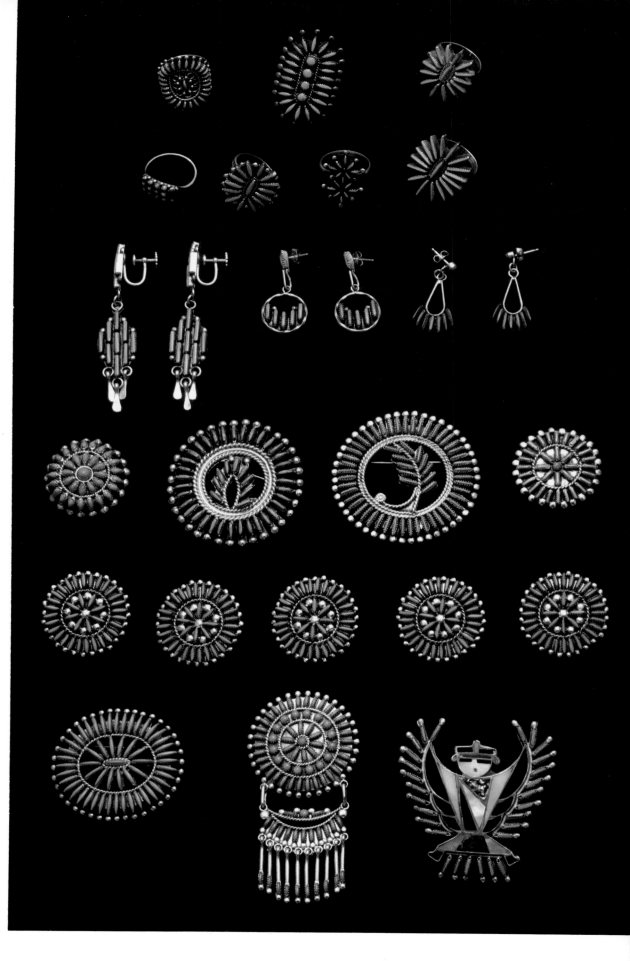

Etched inlay belt buckles made in 1991. **Row 1**: (*From left to right*) Hummingbird made of turquoise, coral, jet, mother-of-pearl, abalone and pink shell by Nichelle and Derrick Edaakie. Blue jay made of turquoise, coral, jet, mother-of-pearl and abalone by Nichelle and Derrick Edaakie. **Row 2**: Cardinal made of Chinese turquoise, coral, jet, mother-of-pearl and gold lip mother-of-pearl by Dolly and Albert Banteah. Eagle made of turquoise, coral, jet, mother-of-pearl and gold lip mother-of-pearl by Nichelle and Derrick Edaakie. **Row 3**: Eagle made of turquoise, coral, jet, mother-of-pearl, gold lip mother-of-pearl and malachite by Rolanda and Harlan Coonsis. Steller's jay made of turquoise, coral, jet, mother-of-pearl and malachite by Esther and Sammy Guardian. Courtesy of Turquoise Village. $225-$900

Belt buckles made in 1991. **Row 1**: (*From left to right*) Mosaic inlay made of turquoise, coral, jet, mother-of-pearl and gold lip mother-of-pearl by Lorenda and Edison Bobelu. Inlay made of turquoise, coral, jet and mother-of-pearl by Earlene Bowannie. **Row 2**: Inlay and raised inlay Apache Mountain Spirit Dancers made of turquoise, coral, jet, mother-of-pearl and melon shell by Tony Ohmsatte. Inlay in a rug pattern made of turquoise, coral, jet, mother-of-pearl and green snail shell by Charlotte Dishta and Pat Leekity. **Row 3**: Inlay Thunderbird made of turquoise, coral, mother-of-pearl and penn shell by Corraine and Bobby Shack. Inlay with Sun God made of turquoise, coral, jet, gold lip mother-of-pearl, lapis lazuli, sugilite and malachite by Ernie Ohmsatte. Courtesy of Turquoise Village. $225-450

BELT BUCKLES

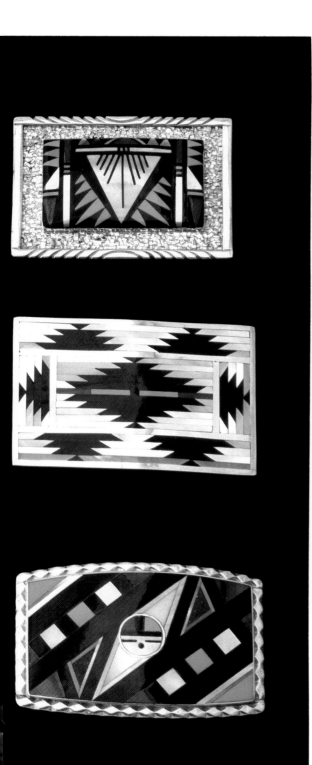

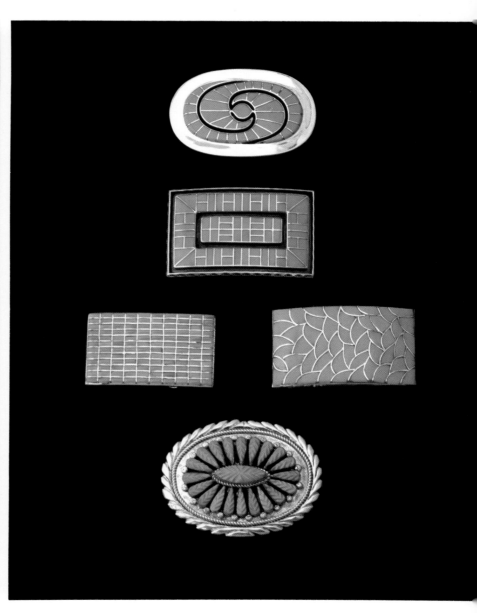

Turquoise belt buckles made in 1991. **Row 1**: (*From top to bottom*) Oval channel inlay made by Amy Wesley. **Row 2**: Channel inlay made by Nancy and Sheldon Westika. **Row 3**: Channel inlay made by Gloria Tucson. Channel inlay made by Margie and Stuart Tucson. **Row 4**: Carved raised turquoise made by Robert Eustace. Courtesy of Turquoise Village. $225-$600

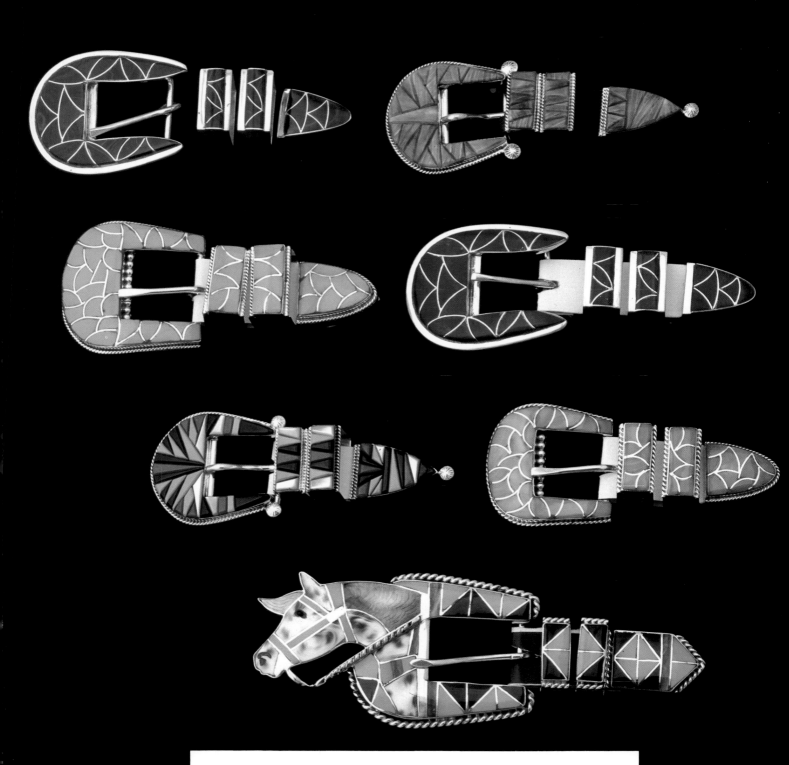

Belt Buckles made in 1991. **Row 1**: (*From left to right*) Channel inlay made of malachite by Orlinda Natewa. Inlay made of red spiny oyster shell by Gladys and Leslie Lamy. **Row 2**: Channel inlay made of turquoise by Margie and Stuart Tucson. Channel inlay made of lapis lazuli by Orlinda Natewa. **Row 3**: Raised inlay made of turquoise, coral, jet and green snail shell by Gladys and Leslie Lamy. Channel inlay made of pink coral by Margie and Stuart Tucson. **Row 4**: Channel inlay of a horse made of turquoise, jet, spiny oyster shell, cowrie shell and black lip oyster shell by Helen and Lincoln Zunie. Courtesy of Turquoise Village. $225-$450

EARRINGS

Turquoise earrings made in 1991. **Row 1:** *(From left to right)* Needlepoint made by Vernon Peynetsa. Petit point hoop made by Bernard Cachini. **Row 2:** Needlepoint made by Dewey Ghahate. Petit point made by Arlene Cellicion. Snake eyes hoop made by Alice and Tom Hannaweeka. **Row 3:** Needlepoint. Artist unknown. Snake eyes made by Lewis Malie. **Row 4:** Needlepoint made by Rena and Evans Waatsa. Snake eyes and round dots made by Arlene Dosedo. Courtesy of Turquoise Village. $25-$75

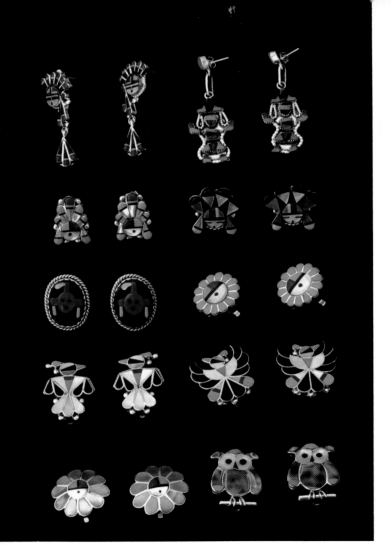

Earrings made in 1991. **Row 1**: *(From left to right)* Raised inlay of Sun God with eagle feathers made of turquoise, coral, jet and mother-of-pearl made by Geraldine Lonjose and Danford Gchachu. Inlay of Knife Wing Dancer made of turquoise, coral and jet by Serena Johnson. **Row 2**: Raised inlay of Sun God with eagle feathers made of turquoise, coral, jet and mother-of-pearl by Geraldine Lonjose. Inlay of Sun God with eagle feathers made of turquoise, coral, jet, mother-of-pearl and pink shell by Patty and Rayland Edaakie. **Row 3**: Inlay of Mudhead Kachina made of turquoise, coral, jet, mother-of-pearl and penn shell by Judy Calavaza. Inlay of turquoise, coral, jet and mother-of-pearl by Phyllis and Lincoln Lonjose. **Row 4**: Inlay of Thunderbird made of turquoise, coral, jet and mother-of-pearl by Faye Tsosie. Inlay of Knife Wing Dancer made of turquoise, coral, jet and mother-of-pearl by Sonny Wallace. **Row 5**: Inlay of coved Sun God made of turquoise, coral, jet, mother-of-pearl and pink shell by Ashbury Gasper. Raised inlay of owl made of cowrie shell, turquoise, jet and white clam shell by Deanne and Elloyd Qualo. Courtesy of Turquoise Village. $35-$75

Coral and pink coral earrings made in 1991. **Row 1**: *(From left to right)* Inlay with jet made by KRS. Inlay made by Margarita Chavez. Inlay made by Olivia Nastacio. Inlay with jet made by Kristen Bowannie. Petit point and round dots made by Marcie Stead. Cluster made by Patsy Weebothee. **Row 2**: Channel inlay made by Stuart Quandelacy. Petit point made by Margarita Chavez. Channel inlay with jet made by Emma Paquin. Petit point made by Margarita Chavez. Dots made by Wilbur Siutza. **Row 3**: Dangle made by Arvina Pinto. One-stone made by Smith Cachini. Cluster made by Lou and Bill Laweka. One-stone made by Lydia Simplicio. Cluster made by Patsy Weebothee. Courtesy of Turquoise Village. $12-$270

CONCHA BELTS

Inlay butterflies joined to create a concha belt consisting of fourteen conchas, with only two alike. The stones and shells include turquoise, coral, jet, tortoise shell, mother-of-pearl, black lip oyster shell, gold lip mother-of-pearl and pink shell. Made by Reyes Neha in the 1960s. Private collection. *Center:* Ring made of tortoise shell, turquoise and coral by Rosita Wallace in the 1960s. Private collection. *Upper:* pin-pendant and matching ring made of turquoise, coral, jet and mother-of-pearl by Rosita Wallace in the 1980s. Courtesy of Leslie Newman. Pin-pendant made of turquoise, coral, jet and mother-of-pearl by Rosita Wallace in the 1970s. Private collection. $60-$900

Sleeping Beauty turquoise cluster concha belts made in 1991 by Alice Quam. *Left:* Eleven conchas on silver which was the First Prize winner. *Right:* Nine conchas on leather, which was the Second Prize winner. Courtesy of Gallup Inter-Tribal Indian Ceremonial. $5500-$9000

Concha belts made in 1991. *Left*: Turquoise belt in petit point consisting of twenty-one conchas made by Annette Pablito. Center: Turquoise cluster belt consisting of fifteen conchas made by Marsha Dunsworth. *Right*: Inlay belt of Sun God with eagle feathers consisting of sixteen conchas made of jet, turquoise, coral, gold lip mother-of-pearl and mother-of-pearl by Linda and Hubbard Soseeah. Courtesy of Turquoise Village. $390-$900

Etched inlay concha belt, made in 1991, consisting of ten different bird conchas made of turquoise, coral, jet, mother-of-pearl, black lip oyster shell, pink shell, abalone and gold lip mother-of-pearl by Nancy and Ruddell Laconsello which was the First Prize winner. Etched inlay squash blossom necklace and matching earrings with a different bird on each piece made of Chinese turquoise, coral, jet, mother-of-pearl, black lip oyster shell, penn shell, pink shell, lapis lazuli and sugilite by Nancy and Ruddell Laconsello which was the First Prize winner and Best in Category for Inlay and Channel Inlay. Courtesy of Gallup Inter-Tribal Indian Ceremonial. $5400-$6000

Inlay jewelry made in 1991. Bracelet with cardinal made of coral, lapis lazuli, mother-of-pearl, pink shell, gold lip mother-of-pearl, malachite, jet and Chinese turquoise by Nancy and Ruddell Laconsello. Bracelet with cardinal made of coral, lapis lazuli, pink shell, jet, malachite, Chinese turquoise and white clam shell by Nancy and Ruddell Laconsello. Concha belt consisting of twelve conchas each depicting a different bird. The belt was made with Chinese turquoise, coral, malachite, mother-of-pearl, jet, gold lip mother-of-pearl, pink coral, abalone and black lip oyster shell by Rolanda Coonsis. *From the top right, clockwise*: The birds are a bald eagle, ruby-throated hummingbird, mallard, cardinal, blue bunting, blue jay, eastern bluebird, ringneck pheasant, summer tananger, kingfisher, redtailed hawk and scarlet macaw. *Center*: Two-sided pendant of hummingbird design made of turquoise, coral, abalone, jet, malachite, lapis lazuli and mother-of-pearl by Esther and Sammy Guardian. Two-sided pendant of cardinal design made of turquoise, coral, jet, mother-of-pearl, gold lip mother-of-pearl and abalone by Nancy and Dennis Edaakie. Courtesy of Turquoise Village. $600-$3000

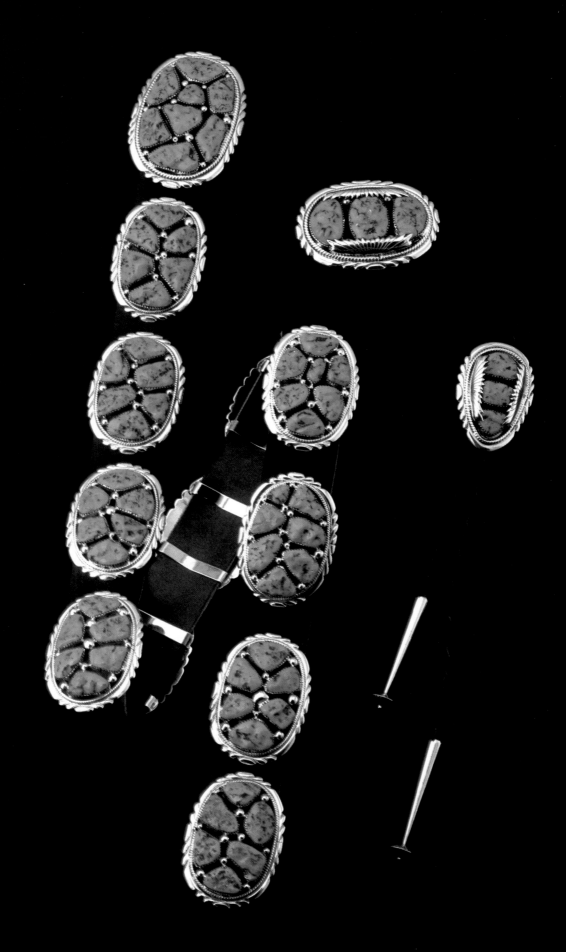

PENDANTS

A two-sided pendant, one side with a Sun God and the other side with a butterfly, made of turquoise, coral, jet, mother-of-pearl, serpentine, abalone, melon shell and black lip oyster shell by Serena and Garrett Banteah in the 1970s. Private collection. $2000

Opposite page:
Concha belt consisting of twelve conchas, a matching belt buckle and bola tie made of Sleeping Beauty turquoise nuggets by Bernice and Robert Leekya in 1991. Courtesy of Turquoise Village. $4000-$4500 set.

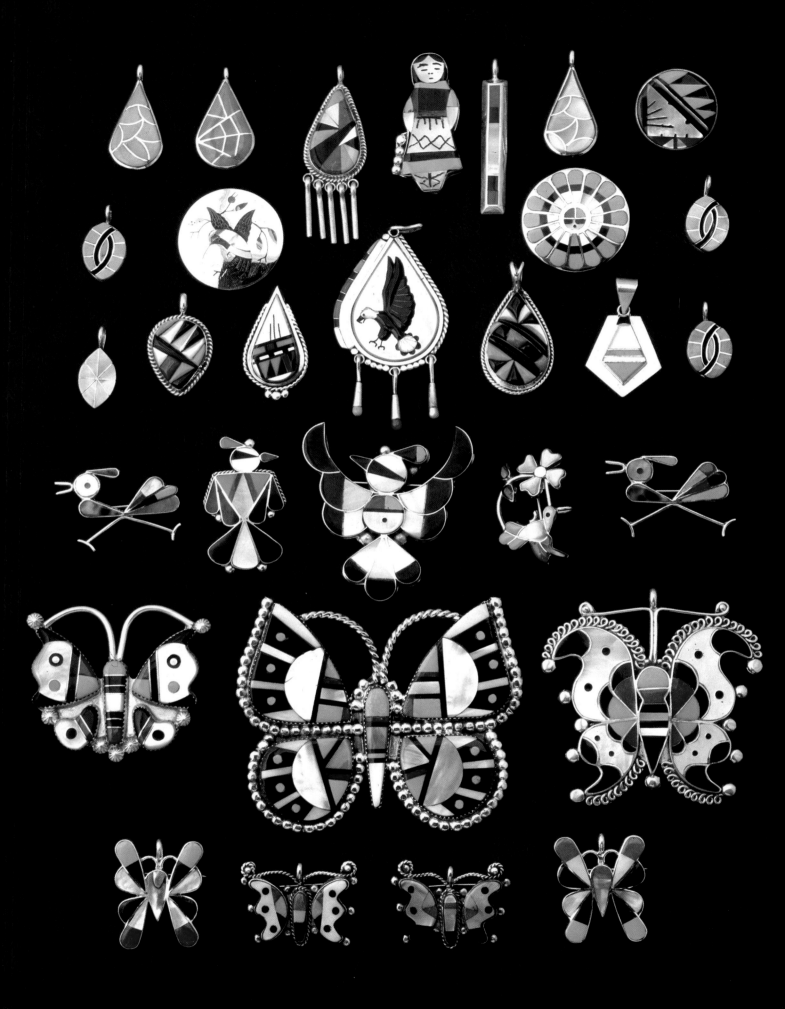

Opposite page:

A variety of pendants made in 1991. **Row 1**: (*From left to right*) Turquoise channel inlay made by Thurza Leekya. Pink coral channel inlay made by Marcie and Laurie Kallestewa. Inlay made of mother-of-pearl, coral, turquoise, gold lip mother-of-pearl and pink shell by Gladys and Leslie Lamy. Inlay of Zuni Maiden made of turquoise, coral, jet and mother-of-pearl by Theresa Waseta. Inlay made of coral, jet and pink shell by Troy Natachu. Channel inlay made of pink shell by Thurza Leekya. Inlay made of turquoise, coral, jet, pink shell and gold lip mother-of-pearl by Marlene and Charles Booqua. **Row 2**: Turquoise channel inlay made by Virginia Laiteyice. Etched inlay of hummingbird made of coral, jet, mother-of-pearl and lapis lazuli by Jane and Myron Edaakie. Raised inlay of eagle made of turquoise, coral, jet, mother-of-pearl and gold lip mother-of-pearl by Don C. Dewa. Inlay Sun God made of turquoise, coral, jet and gold lip mother-of-pearl by Jenelle and Keith Waatsa. Pink coral channel inlay made by Virginia Laiteyice. **Row 3**: Pink shell channel inlay made by Alberta Espino. Raised inlay made of turquoise, coral, jet and mother-of-pearl by Gladys and Leslie Lamy. Inlay made of turquoise, coral, jet and gold lip mother-of-pearl by Erlinda and Ardale Mahooty. Raised inlay made of turquoise, jet and gold lip mother-of-pearl by Lolita Milani. Inlay made of turquoise and gold lip mother-of-pearl by Wilda and Jan Boone. Pink coral channel inlay made by Virginia Laiteyice. **Row 4**: Inlay of roadrunner made of turquoise, coral, jet, mother-of-pearl, cowrie shell and pink shell by Maryjane Edaakie. Inlay of Thunderbird made of turquoise, coral, jet and mother-of-pearl by Clifford Bowannie. Inlay of Thunderbird with Sun God made of turquoise, coral, jet and mother-of-pearl by Yvonne and Felix Charlie. Raised inlay of hummingbird with flower made of turquoise, coral, mother-of-pearl, gold lip mother-of-pearl and malachite by Valerie and Pasco Comosone. Inlay of roadrunner made of turquoise, coral, jet, mother-of-pearl, gold lip mother-of-pearl and cowrie shell by Maryjane Edaakie. **Row 5**: Raised inlay of butterfly made of turquoise, coral, jet and gold lip mother-of-pearl by Elvira Leekity. Raised inlay of butterfly made of turquoise, coral, jet, gold lip mother-of-pearl and pink shell by Angela and Oliver Cellicion. Inlay of butterfly made of turquoise, coral, jet and mother-of-pearl by Loren Leekela. **Row 6**: Inlay of butterfly made of turquoise, coral, gold lip mother-of-pearl, pink shell and abalone by Sarah Edaakie. Raised inlay of butterfly made of turquoise, coral, jet and white clam shell by Verdie Booqua. Raised inlay of butterfly made of turquoise, coral, jet and pink shell by Verdie Booqua. Inlay of butterfly made of turquoise, coral, jet, mother-of-pearl, pink shell and abalone by Sarah Edaakie. Courtesy of Turquoise Village. $18-$375

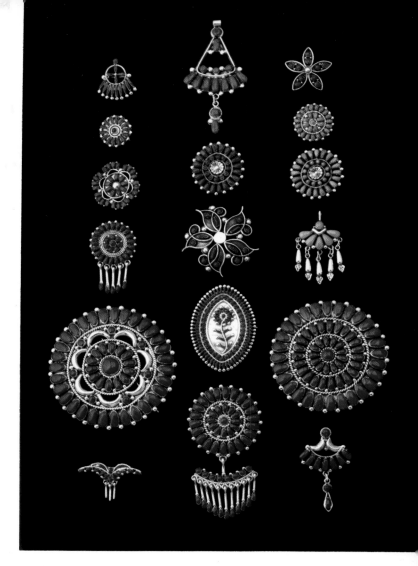

Coral and pink coral pendants made of needlepoint, petit point, cluster and snake eyes in 1991. The artists whose work is represented are: **Row 1**: Ruby Gchachu, Shirley Lahi, Marylou and Joe Quampahone, Rosanda Quatawki, Alice Quam, and Alice Mutte. **Row 2**: Lou and Bill Laweka, Marcie Stead, Bernadine Charlie, Socorro and Vincent Johnson, and Lorraine and Luwayne Waatsa. **Row 3**: Bernadine Charlie, Lucita Bobelu, Marcie Stead, Beverly Weebothee, Alice Quam, and Lou and Bill Laweka. Courtesy of Turquoise Village. $30-$900

Turquoise pendants made of needlepoint, petit point, cluster and snake eyes in 1991. The artists whose work is represented are Patrick Chavez, Antonita Pattone, Lou and Bill Laweka, Delbert Booqua, Hubert Johnson, Edison Yatsattie, Floyd Etsate, Patsy Weebothee, Beverly Etsate, Arlita and Philip Lahi, Henderson Soseeah, Danny Etsate, Joanne Lalio, Odelle and Alex Seowtewa, Kristen Bowannie, Rena and Evans Waatsa, Caroline Eriacho, Stanley Awelagte, Georgeanne Pencion, Beverly Weebothee, Elaine Luarkie, Rose Gchachu, Mary and Lee Weebothee, Marylou Quampahone, and Maryann and Felix Chavez. Courtesy of Turquoise Village. $30-$300

MATCHING SETS

The Lone Mountain needlepoint necklace and earrings made by Edith Tsabetsaye in 1990 was the First Prize winner at the Gallup Inter-Tribal Indian Ceremonial that year. Courtesy of Roxanne and Greg Hofmann. $10,500 set.

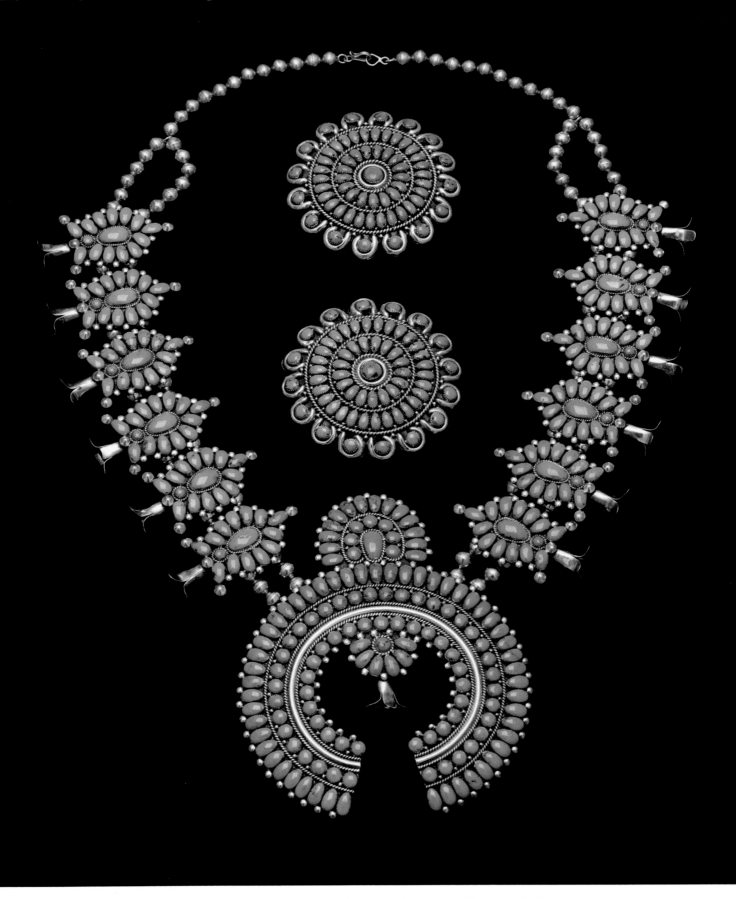

Lone Mountain turquoise cluster squash blossom necklace made in 1968 and two pins made of Lone Mountain turquoise in 1972 by Edith Tsabetsaye, from her collection. $5000 set.

Inlay Sun God squash blossom necklace, earrings and link bracelet made of turquoise, coral, jet and mother-of-pearl in the 1970s by Sadie and Morris Laahty. Private collection. $2000-$2500 set.

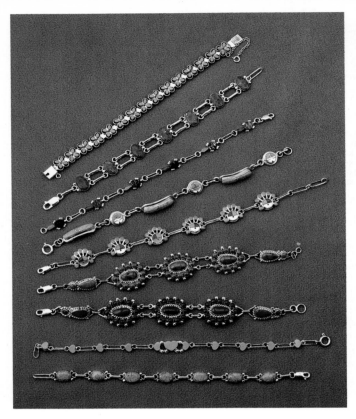

Link bracelets made in 1998. *From top to bottom:* Turquoise made by Janice Lonjose. Denim lapis lazuli made by Diane Lonjose. Turquoise, coral, malachite, abalone, and orange, red, and purple spiny oyster shell turtles made by Lynette Chuyate. Mother-of-pearl, gaspeite, and jet inlay sun faces made by Patty and Raylan Edaakie. Turquoise, coral, mother-of-pearl, and jet inlay sun faces made by Vernelda Niiha. Chinese turquoise cluster made by Lorraine and Luwayne Waatsa. Coral cluster made by Lorraine and Luwayne Waatsa. Turquoise hearts made by Harriet Johnson. Gaspeite made by Diane Lonjose. Courtesy of Turquoise Village. $36-$435

Belt buckles made in 1998. **Row 1:** *(From left to right)* Turquoise and branch coral made by Robert and Bernice Leekya. **Row 2:** Turquoise made by Wayne Cheama. Raised turquoise made by Alvina Quam. **Row 3:** Turquoise, coral, yellow, white, gold lip mother-of-pearl, and jet inlay made by Marlene Booqua. Turquoise, coral, mother-of-pearl, and jet inlay made by Herbert Kallestewa. **Row 4:** Turquoise, coral, mother-of-pearl, and jet inlay made by Maderral Kallestewa. Courtesy of Turquoise Village. $105-$450

Necklaces made in 1998. *From top to bottom:* Coral needlepoint and earrings with silver dangles made by Stewart and Jocelyn Nakatewa. Turquoise petit point made by Rosemary Panteah. Coral round stones and earrings made by Glenda Eriacho. Coral with silver stamped dangles and earrings made by Norbert and Florinda Haskie. Courtesy of Turquoise Village. $255-$450

Bracelets made in 1998. **Row 1:** *(From left to right)* Coral petit point made by Eunice Lunasee. **Row 2:** Turquoise needlepoint made by Bryant Waatsa, Sr. Turquoise cluster made by Martha Toshowna. **Row 3:** Turquoise needlepoint made by Shirley Quam. Turquoise petit point made by Eunice Lunasee. **Row 4:** Turquoise petit point made by Norman and Virginia Hooee. Coral petit point with needlepoint stone in center made by Judy Wallace. **Row 5:** Turquoise needlepoint made by Danny Etsate. Courtesy of Turquoise Village. $60-$255